Praise for
What the Happiest Retirees Know and Wes Moss

Successful aging is not just about adding more years to your life but, rather, adding life to your years. Through his research, Moss has identified the essential lifestyle habits of those who want to retire happily yet still be engaged with life. This is a must-read for anyone who wants to optimize their Third Act in life.

—Dan Buettner, National Geographic Fellow and #1 *New York Times* bestselling author of *The Blue Zones*

I have had so much fun reading Wes's latest book. What the happiest retirees know that *you* need to learn are a lot of things about money but, more importantly, how you live your life. You expect you need to have saved enough to cover your retirement years. Wes proves that only gets you part of the way. Relationships, family, hobbies, volunteering, and being involved in community are central to your happiness. Read this and you will be on your way to a full, rewarding retirement life.

—Clark Howard, consumer advocate, money expert, and *New York Times* bestselling author of *Living Large in Lean Times*

I have studied retirement for many years. Well written and very engaging, this book is one of the best I have read on this topic. Moss has made a major contribution to the understanding of and planning for retirement. His examples are not only entertaining but extremely informative. This book is for everyone, no matter what stage they are at in their careers.

—Louis H. Primavera, PhD, Dean of the School of Health Sciences of Touro College and author of *The Retirement Maze*

I've been in the retirement services industry for more than two decades, and in that time, I've read a myriad of books on retirement. This book does what others do not in that it gives actionable strategies for having a happier, more fulfilling life in retirement. Moss not only provides sound financial advice but also reveals the social and emotional traits of the happiest retirees in the world. If you want to plan for a satisfying retirement, read this book.

—Richard Tatum, President of Retirement Services at Vestwell

Thanks to this great new book, Wes Moss has convinced me that I've done almost everything wrong with my own financial planning. The good news is that it's not too late for me—or you. Using the advice laid out in these pages, you'll be able to retire sooner and wealthier.

—Eric Von Haessler, host of
The Von Haessler Doctrine on WSB Radio

WHAT THE
Happiest
Retirees
Know

Other Books by Wes Moss

You Can Retire Sooner Than You Think

Starting from Scratch

WHAT THE
Happiest
Retirees
Know

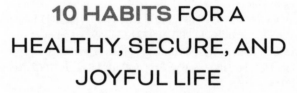

10 HABITS FOR A
HEALTHY, SECURE, AND
JOYFUL LIFE

Wes Moss

Mc Graw Hill

NEW YORK CHICAGO SAN FRANCISCO ATHENS LONDON
MADRID MEXICO CITY MILAN NEW DELHI
SINGAPORE SYDNEY TORONTO

1 2 3 4 5 6 7 8 9   LCR   26 25 24 23 22 21

ISBN   978-1-264-26926-6
MHID   1-264-26926-9

e-ISBN   978-1-264-26927-3
e-MHID   1-264-26927-7

Design by Lee Fukui and Mauna Eichner

Library of Congress Cataloging-in-Publication Data

Name: Moss, Wes, author.
Title: What the happiest retirees know : 10 habits for a healthy, secure, and joyful life / Wes Moss.
Description: New York : McGraw Hill, 2022. | Includes bibliographical references and index.
Identifiers: LCCN 2021027840 (print) | LCCN 2021027841 (ebook) | ISBN 9781264269266 (hardback) | ISBN 9781264269273 (ebook)
Subjects: LCSH: Retirement—Planning. | Finance, Personal.
Classification: LCC HQ1062 .M656 2021 (print) | LCC HQ1062 (ebook) | DDC 332.024/014—dc23
LC record available at https://lccn.loc.gov/2021027840
LC ebook record available at https://lccn.loc.gov/2021027841

McGraw Hill books are available at special quantity discounts to use as premiums and sales promotions or for use in corporate training programs. To contact a representative, please visit the Contact Us pages at www.mhprofessional.com.

To my wife, Lynne, who talked me into having more than 2.5 children, and our boys Ben, Luke, Jake, and Samuel, who bring true happiness to us and the world around them.

Contents

CONTENTS

Preface

When I was five years old, my father, a large-animal veterinarian, took me out on farm calls with him. We lived about 15 minutes from the mecca of Amish Americans—Lancaster County, Pennsylvania—and most of my dad's clients were Amish.

The Amish are a group of traditionalist Christian fellowships with Swiss German Anabaptist origins, known for simple living, plain dress, and a strong aversion to modern technology. They're often represented in movies dressed like pilgrims and riding in horse-drawn buggies. Pop culture has long been fascinated with the Amish—take the 1985 movie *Witness*, which starred post–Han Solo Harrison Ford and pre–*Top Gun* Kelly McGillis in a bonnet. More recently, *Breaking Amish*, a reality TV series, followed four young Amish adults and one Mennonite through their adventures in New York City.

From ages 5 to 10, I spent a lot of time on those Amish farms, making the short trek there in my dad's red pickup truck—the one with the little hatch attached to the back cab window that held all his medical tools—to treat dairy cows for milk fever. On a typical call, particularly in the summer, my dad would care for anywhere from 10 to 20 cows. That took several hours, which meant I was stuck there. So what did I do?

I got to know that world.

The Amish have no electricity, no means of fast and convenient communication, no cars. I'll never forget how excited my

Amish friends were to climb into my dad's truck and listen to the radio. These days, when I'm hosting *Money Matters* on News-Talk WSB Radio, the country's longest-running live call-in investment-and-personal-finance radio show, I sometimes wonder if one of them is out there, listening in someone else's dad's pickup truck. I'd be honored.

I got so close to the Amish kids that they'd invite me to go fish gigging. What is fish gigging? I didn't know, either—it's basically taking a three-pronged spear and hunting for fish. Picture Poseidon holding his trident. Now turn that Greek god into a lanky blond kid and three boys in suspenders. That was our fish-gigging crew, and it was wonderful.

At night we'd take gaslit lanterns, wander through the streams that cut across the pastures, and thrust those tridents at the suckers and flounders. Then we'd toss our catch into a feed sack, take them home, and eat fried fish with terrible-tasting ketchup. The life experience was delicious.

Those Amish farms got me thinking about the haves and have-nots of happiness. I lived with my parents and brothers in a middle-class area out near horse country. Land was cheap, but it was what you might call "rich-neighborhood adjacent." I didn't have to go far to come across wealthy folks sitting on 500 acres with a dozen horses grazing on premium-quality grass. Every day, I saw luxury and opulence.

Then my dad would take me to Amish country. And suddenly, I'd find myself in the middle of an old-fashioned world where people had zero modern amenities—by *choice*. My dad worked tirelessly to help these humble farmers, men and women living in much the same way as their forebears did 300 years ago. And here's what I observed:

They seemed happy.

At the time, I sensed a sharp contrast between the two groups—the wealthy folks and the Amish, the so-called "haves" and "have-nots"—but I couldn't quite put my finger on *why*. Were the rich folks happy? If so, was it because they were rich? Were the Amish families happy? Were they and their milk-fevered cows happier than the rich people riding around on their 17 Lipizzan stallions?

I knew the answer even before I'd officially asked the question. The Amish farmers, who ostensibly had very little, were clearly just as happy—or even happier—than the wealthy folks.

But *why*?

What a lot of people don't know about the Amish is that they are pretty savvy business operators. Though they live simply, they are hardworking farmers and builders, and they know how to make a decent living. My family had a couple of barns, and both were built—and built well—by Amish people. They knew how to get jobs and land repeat business. They didn't have fancy new cars and designer clothes, but that was by choice, not circumstance.

As a kid, I took all this in. It coalesced into a single question:

Does money buy happiness?

The Amish seemed to be living well enough. Not high on the hog, but *medium* on the hog, at least. I knew there was no way they had as much money as my neighbor with the three tennis courts and gold-plated bidet, but they seemed happier. So the question evolved into:

How exactly does money correlate to happiness?

That question grew into a passion, then an obsession, and then a career. My early days on Amish farms were the beginning of a journey that took me from pursuing a degree in economics from the University of North Carolina, Chapel Hill, to becoming the chief investment strategist at Capital Investment Advisors (CIA), to hosting the *Money Matters* radio show, to writing *You Can Retire*

Sooner Than You Think: The 5 Money Secrets of the Happiest Retirees, to creating the Retire Sooner podcast, and ultimately, here: writing my next book, this time about the 10 habits of the happiest retirees.

This book has been more than 10 years in the making. In 2010, I read an article in *Time* magazine that had a powerful impact on me:[1] Princeton University had published a study showing that once people reach an income in the neighborhood of $75,000 per year, happiness levels off.[2] The further you fell below $75,000, the more unhappy you were, but rising *above* $75,000 led to diminishing returns of happiness. So $75,000 per year per household seemed to be the magic number.

The results of that study rattled around in my cerebral can as the world continued to deal with the fallout of the 2008 financial crisis. At the time, I was beginning to notice certain trends in conversations with some of the families I advised. They were calmer. They emerged from the crisis with fewer financial losses—and a lot less anger and anxiety than their peers. In other words: *they were happier*.

Why them? What did they *know*? What did they *do*?

That's when I decided to conduct my first intensive study on the relationship between money and happiness. That study led to a large data set of unconventional financial rules that effectively showed me the habits of happy retirees relative to unhappy ones, and compelled me to write *You Can Retire Sooner Than You Think*. The idea of reverse-engineering happiness from a money standpoint appealed to me, so I took the habits of happy retirees and drilled down on what they were doing, pouring that information straight into the book.

Now, over a decade later, I've come to realize just how powerful and important those habits are. There is a lot of negative and just-plain-wrong information around retiring, even from reputable sources such as the *Wall Street Journal*. While the *Journal* is one of my most trusted sources of financial news, it's not right about everything—and certainly not when it made its "Case Against Early Retirement" in 2019.[3]

That article became my nemesis. As soon as I read it, I knew I had to rebut it. I don't want you to become another one of *WSJ*'s scary statistics. That was just one of many reasons I decided to expand and deepen my research, compiling it into a new book.

I conducted another study, this one geared toward specific lifestyle habits of happy versus unhappy retirees. I had already mined for gold by asking, "How much money does it take to be happy?" Now I was ready to go spelunking, dropping deep into the lifestyle traits, activities, and behaviors happy retirees had in common. I knew there was more precious metal in those caverns, and I was determined to unearth it.

That's what this book is about. We are going to build on the core financial traits—the good money habits of happy retirees— and then look at them through a wider lens. Because happiness isn't only about how much money retirees have. It's about what they do with it—and what that money is *for*.

This book will show you the decisions and choices the happiest retirees are making, as well as the behaviors and pursuits they've adopted, so that you can emulate them in your own life.

Let's take my father as an example. At 67 years old, he is a very happy retiree. A veterinarian for 43 of those years, he'd come a long way from his days as the dairy-cow whisperer of Amish country. When he decided to sell his practice, he sent the following letter to his clients with a picture enclosed (Figure P.1):

Dear Friends and Pets,

It was June 1976 when I first began practicing veterinary medicine with Dr. James Cowan at the Brandywine Valley Veterinary Hospital. The past 43 years have been extremely fulfilling for me personally, starting with a James-Herriot type practice working with Amish dairy farms and small animals, then evolving into the sophisticated medical and surgical practice that it is today.

The time has come for me to pass the torch on to another. This November, I will no longer be the owner of the hospital. I have sold the practice to Dr. Marc Daniel, who I believe will continue to serve you and your pets with the same concern and passion you have come to expect from us.

I must admit that I approach this change of life with mixed emotions. While stepping away from veterinary medicine is hard, as many of you know I have a few other interests that I look forward to pursuing (**geology, Civil War medicine, fencing, leatherwork, fox hunting, trail riding, woodworking, sewing, time-traveling through historical reenacting, music, art, cooking, blacksmithing, cowboy poetry, and more!**) I am also looking forward to spending more time with our family (four grown children and eight growing grandchildren) and supporting my wife Anne's interests and career in pottery and equine pursuits.

Reflecting on the last 43 years, I realize what an honor and privilege it has been to assist you and your furry family members with the help of an exceptional team of technicians, veterinary assistants, and receptionists. I appreciate our time together. Thank You for the privilege of the relationships I have had with you and your pets for so many years.

Sincerely,
John T. Moss

FIGURE P.1 **John Moss and grandkids**

Once you've dried your eyes, refocus them on the words in bold (emphasis mine). My dad listed *14 core pursuits*. In other words, 14 activities he enjoys doing that have nothing to do with his career. After a lifetime of passionately caring for animals, he is now caring for himself, forging ahead into new adventures and the next chapter of his life.

We'll talk more about core pursuits later in the book. For now, I'll leave you with this: If John T. Moss can make the leap from Amish dairy farms to time-traveling through historical reenactments and supporting his wife's equine pursuits, imagine what *you* can do. Your life does not end when your career does. It becomes new again, and the opportunities are endless.

My dad made the right financial decisions and saved for his retirement. As my last book pointed out, that is key. But it's only one piece of the puzzle. Even if you have the economic security you need, what good is it if you aren't happy?

One of my most vivid memories of visiting the Amish farms is a less-than-pleasant one. You may not know what a cow gutter is, but it's certainly something I will never forget. A cow gutter is the trough that lines the area where all the cows stand. To put it delicately: it's where all the cow manure goes.

On one Amish farm visit, my childhood self managed to fall into one of these dung ditches. I won't describe the smell, but suffice it to say that was the day I officially decided *not* to become a veterinarian. Any hope my father might have had that his son would follow in his footsteps literally went to shit that day. No thanks!

But I did learn something from my old man. I learned that in order to provide the best of care, every creature must be carefully studied. Rather than studying animals, I chose to study another creature: the happy retiree. Or, as I'll refer to them in these pages, HROBs: the Happiest Retirees on the Block.

What the Happiest Retirees Know is the result of that labor. I'll share dozens of stories from the HROBs I've known and worked with so you can see them in action, living their best lives. They're all happy to share their secrets to success. This is my fan letter to HROBs—and an instruction manual for those who want to achieve the same results. Though I've changed some names and identifying details, their happiness is very real.

This book is also a how-to for anyone who wants to retire early. In the Venn diagram of a fulfilling retirement, the circles for "retire happy" and "retire early" overlap. Think of this book as a kind of time machine. It might not be as stylish as a DeLorean, but it's going to fast-track you to a healthy, secure, and joyful life.

Whether you're still in your thirties or forties projecting ahead into the future, or you're in your fifties or sixties getting ready to retire, or you already *are* retired, I've got good news: these habits, behaviors, lifestyle choices, and financial principles are ones you can adopt today.

And if you're already happy? Great! This book will show you all kinds of ways to keep up the good work. Stay out of the cow gutters—and don't buy that BMW, no matter how much you may think you want to.

I love working with happy retirees. They remind me that a happy, early retirement really is easier than you think. I've learned so much from them.

And now you can, too.

WHAT THE
Happiest
Retirees
Know

CHAPTER 1

Who Is the Happiest Retiree on the Block?

Ron and Rita love their family.

When they call into my radio show, that's the first thing they tell me. "Ron and Rita Margarita," as I affectionately dub them, adore their big family, but they haven't been able to see them for the better part of a year.

"We are lucky in so many ways," Ron says, in his charming Southern drawl. "Rita and I are both very healthy—we ski every winter and do a lot of hiking in the summer—and neither of us has been sick in years. And I can work virtually."

Ron is 62 and a high-level executive at an insurance company. Rita has an Etsy shop where she sells hand-carved wooden keepsakes and knickknacks. She's a freshly minted 60.

"I turned 29 last month," she says, and I can practically hear the wink in her voice. "It just so happens that I've turned 29 thirty-two times."

"We're big fans of *Money Matters*," Ron says. "We called because we need your advice. Now that America is opening up again, we want to do something big to celebrate! We're dying to see our kids and grandkids because, to put it bluntly: we miss 'em like hell."

Ron and Rita proceed to tell me all the exciting family news about their four adult kids: Their youngest son, Les, proposed to his longtime girlfriend, Debbie, and they're happily planning their wedding. The Margaritas' eldest son, Greg, works in tech and got an impressive job offer from a competing startup. Buoyed by his new salary, Greg, his wife, Cathy, and their four kids moved to the Midwest. Then there's Ron and Rita's eldest daughter, Christine, a nurse and frontline worker. "A hero," Ron tells me, "with the formidable immune system of a mom of three." And their youngest daughter, Laurie, just gave birth to her first son with husband Steve.

"Want to hear the clincher?" Ron asks. "In a few months we'll be celebrating our fortieth wedding anniversary."

"And as much as I love one-on-one time with Ron," Rita says wryly, "I wouldn't mind celebrating with friends and family, too."

"That's why we called you," Ron says. "We want to plan a big ole family reunion."

"Our dream is to invite our four kids, their partners, and all the grandkids to our favorite resort in Sandy Springs for a weekend extravaganza," says Rita. "And then open it up on the second night to friends. But the thing is, Ron is planning to retire in the next few years, and my Etsy shop is mostly for fun. We're nervous about spending a big chunk of money."

"Understood," I say. "Talk to me about your retirement planning."

As Ron and Rita Margarita walk me through their financial strategies and decisions, it quickly becomes apparent they've done pretty much everything right. They have roughly a million in net worth—$500,000 in retirement and IRAs, $600,000 in investments in brokerage accounts (from savings and inheritance), and the remaining amount in real estate. They live in a nice house in Marietta, Georgia—not a mansion, but nice—and they paid off their mortgage 10 years ago. Their kids are financially independent. Two stayed in Georgia and two live out of state, but all four are out in the world with good jobs, raising families of their own.

Ron drives a Lexus, and Rita loves her 2020 Toyota Highlander. They typically go on a nice trip or cruise twice a year, and they alternate who gets to pick their destination. Last year, Rita chose the Italian Riviera. The year before that, Ron chose Timbuktu.

When I commend them on making excellent financial decisions, Ron says, "Well, of course, Wes, we are happy retirees!"

I smile. They can't see it, because this is radio.

"Let's break down what this epic reunion event would cost," I say.

Together, we do the math. The Margaritas are looking at hosting 16 people: four kids, three spouses, a fiancée, and eight grandkids. Plane tickets are an average of $400 apiece, so that's $6,400 for airfare. We'll say five hotel rooms, because Greg and Cathy have two teenagers and Christine has one—the three cousins will enjoy having their own space. Let's just hope they don't get into too much trouble.

Five hotel rooms for three nights at $250/night comes to $3,750. So we're at roughly $10,000 for hotel and airfare.

Then there's the epic event itself. The Margaritas want to rent the resort ballroom for two nights. The first night is the family-only reunion, so Ron and Rita plus 16 guests. For the second night, they want to pull out all the stops and do their fortieth wedding anniversary right. They're planning to invite friends and extended family, so are expecting 50 to 70 folks.

Basically, they are throwing two mini-weddings. When you add up the rental fee, the catering, and the DJ, it comes out to around $20,000 a night.

"We didn't even spend that much on our *actual* wedding," Rita confides.

"Forty years ago," Ron says wistfully, "we were just a coupla kids with small pocketbooks and big dreams."

I commend Ron on being a poet, and then I say exactly what they've been hoping I'd say:

"Do it."

"Really?" Rita sounds a little giddy. "It's that easy?"

"Look, you two," I answer, and then I put on my best radio-host-and-author voice. "I wouldn't endorse you throwing the reunion bash of the century if I didn't think you could afford it. But you can reward yourself. Do you know why? Because you're HROBs."

There's silence on the other end of the line.

"Uh, Wes?" Ron asks, tentatively. "Remind us what HROBs are again?"

My grin is big enough to fill the resort ballroom in Sandy Springs.

"Ron, I'm so glad you asked."

And then, because this stuff fires me up more than just about anything, I proceed to tell them all about the 10 habits of the Happiest Retirees on the Block.

1. **HROBs have excellent money habits.** They have $500,000 or more in savings, their mortgage payoff is complete (or at least in sight), and they have multiple streams of income.

2. **Happy retirees are curious and adventurous, with at least three core pursuits.** They know how to travel, play,

and explore, and they engage wholeheartedly in three or more hobbies on a regular basis.

3. **They love their kids and see them regularly—but their kids are independent.** The happiest retirees' adult children are out in the world living their own lives, rather than suckling off the financial teats of their parents.

4. **HROBs are married, and they've either never been divorced, or only divorced once.** That's right: you get one marriage do-over.

5. **The happiest retirees believe, give, and do good.** Their faith is important to them, and they go to church at least twice a year. They also volunteer and support the causes they believe in.

6. **HROBs stay connected.** They are, at heart, social creatures. On average they have three close social connections, belong to at least one organized social group, and travel at least once a year with friends.

7. **Happy retirees are healthy.** They are often "on the move," recognizing the value of regular exercise. They are also mindful of what they eat and stick to a health-conscious diet.

8. **HROBs have good home habits.** They don't live in McMansions, they don't have mortgages, and they don't rush to downsize their houses—because they know their kids and grandkids are going to come home to visit.

9. **The happiest retirees exhibit excellent investor behavior.** They don't go chasing waterfalls—by which I mean the investment advice du jour. Even when other retirees default to fight or flight, HROBs remain stoically invested over a long period of time.

10. **They are "masters of the middle."** HROBs are smart spenders. Sure, they may have had times in their lives when they were carrying a little too much credit card debt or struggling financially. But for the most part, they've prioritized saving over spending—and they don't deprive themselves needlessly.

"Whoa now," says Ron. "Hold your horses there, Wes. You rattled those 10 habits off so fast I couldn't write 'em all down."

"Ron likes to keep track of everything," Rita teases, "except for his car keys."

"Well, I can't help with the car keys," I say. "But you're in luck. I'm writing a new book about these 10 overarching financial and lifestyle habits, and the smaller habits inside each one."

"I can't wait to read it," Rita says. "Will you talk about HROBs like us?"

"Just like you," I say and smile.

I WANT TO BE AN HROB!

Who wouldn't want to be an HROB? Maybe you *are* one. If not, you almost certainly know one. I know thousands myself. After all, I've been studying them for years.

The question is, how do you become an HROB—and how do you avoid being a UROB, the Unhappiest Retiree on the Block?

If you read my last book, you know I conducted an extensive survey of retirees nationwide. This time around, I'm back with even bigger, better data. I enlisted the help of nearly 2,000 American retirees, asking them 35 questions about their habits and behaviors. To further the research, I conducted an additional survey in 2021 specific to habits regarding social connectedness.

The surveys got personal. No topic was off limits, even the ones we're not "supposed" to talk about. I asked about money, social media, sex, love, faith, diet—and got some very candid responses. It was everything I could have imagined. Once I crunched the numbers, the results were educational, revealing, and often eye-opening.

Best of all: *the habits were reproducible.* Anyone can do this stuff.

And here's the extra good news. I believe these lifestyle and financial habits aren't just going to help you retire happier: they're going to help you retire *sooner.* The vast majority of the HROBs you'll meet in the following pages were able to retire early *and* happy. These habits, by their very nature, can significantly expedite your retirement timeline—and in so doing, transform your life.

That's why I'm so fired up about the work I do. According to the Financial Planning Association, only *18 percent of US households* have enough wealth to cover preretirement consumption when they retire, meaning most Americans will not be able to maintain their preretirement lifestyle in retirement.[1] That's fewer than one in five people who can retire happy, healthy, and financially secure. To make matters worse, only around half of Americans are actively saving for their golden years.[2] I don't mean to scare you with those statistics—but they are pretty scary. Very few people are prepared for the full retirement journey, and many don't think they will ever be able to quit working.

So if you are able to retire even one year sooner, secure in the knowledge that your money is going to last, then we've accomplished something. If you retire two or three years sooner, it's going to have dramatic repercussions. I've also worked with folks by phone, on Zoom, and in my office who have retired *many* years sooner—maybe a full five or six years before they'd ever imagined they could.

But even if it's just one year, that's huge. Retiring 12 months early is going to have a massive, enduring impact on your life. Imagine a whole extra year of freedom, happiness, health, security, and joy.

Now widen your scope. Think bigger. What if your spouse could also retire sooner? Your twin sister? Your buddy at work? Your neighbor? Your kids? My goal is to help one million Americans retire at least one year sooner. It's why I wrote this book, and also why I launched my new podcast, aptly named: Retire Sooner. I want to create *one million years of financial freedom and retirement joyfulness*.

That is a big number. It's hard to even put that into context as a human being. A million years ago, we were basically running around half naked, trying to get away from woolly mammoths and saber-toothed cats. A lot can happen in a millennium.

Fast-forward to today. So what are these world-altering HROB habits, you ask?

To which I answer: read the book.

But in the meantime . . . here's a little teaser of what's to come.

SHOW ME THE MONEY

Let's start with money. The results are in: the happiest retirees achieve certain financial milestones. For those of you who've read *You Can Retire Sooner Than You Think*, you'll no doubt recognize the three core money habits. These haven't changed, and as far as I'm concerned, they never will.

To refresh your memory, the Happiest Retirees on the Block have:

1. **$500,000 or more in savings.** That's $500,000 per household, not per person. Either a single person living alone or a couple need to hit the $500,000 mark. That number might sound intimidating, but it's actually a doable goal, one that we'll address in Chapter 3. The trick is to figure out how much money you need to save (happiness by liquid net worth) while keeping in mind that $500,000 is an important inflection point. Working backward, we can apply the 1,000-Bucks-a-Month Rule. This rule of thumb stipulates that for every thousand dollars in monthly income you want in retirement, you need to have saved $240,000. Five hundred thousand is about twice that, giving you a little more than $2,000 per month.

2. **A mortgage payoff that is complete or within sight.** HROBs are four times more likely to be mortgage free within five years of retirement than unhappy retirees. In light of the dramatic rise in housing prices over the past several years, the average home value for HROBs is $585,000.

3. **Multiple streams of retirement income.** These can include part-time work, part-time consulting, rental income, investment income (various types), Social Security, and pension income. The source doesn't matter nearly as much as the diversity. The shift in mindset, especially for older generations, is to go from being all about that one big W-2–style paycheck to multiple smaller checks.

After these three essential money habits, the happiest retirees showcase a variety of other financial behaviors. They are smart spenders, prioritizing saving over spending. Whether their monthly spending limit is $5,000, $6,000, or $15,000 per month doesn't matter as long as it's affordable and clearly defined. They don't make investment decisions based on emotion, refusing to let fear, greed, panic, or exuberance make them irrational.

If you worry that you've missed the boat or that you're destined to find yourself shipwrecked on UROB shores, I've got good news. There is always something you can do today to improve your odds of happiness in retirement. A study from my fellow investment team at Capital Investment Advisors shows that, from 1980 through 2020, a $10,000 investment in the S&P 500, assuming all dividends were reinvested into the portfolio, grew to over $1.0 million.[3] I'm not talking about one magical stock purchase that climbed to the moon. I'm talking about a highly diversified investment plan that potentially creates a rising source of income for a lifetime.

You might say, "But, Wes, I *didn't* start planning, investing, and saving 40 years ago. Am I not too late?" Not really. If you're 40 or 50 years old, you have *three to four decades* left to invest.

If your brain is saying, "I'm so behind," remember that you have more years of spending ahead of you than you might think. In Chapter 3, I'll share some exciting new scientific developments regarding life expectancy. Think in decades, not years, and you might be pleasantly surprised.

THE FUN STUFF

What about the nonfinancial behaviors of the happiest retirees? What habits did I uncover that weren't specifically about money?

I discovered, over and over, that the happiest retirees are curious. HROBs are curious to explore, to try new things, and to go out and see what they didn't or couldn't see when they were tied to a desk for all those years. My research found that *HROBs have 3.6 core pursuits, versus 1.9 core pursuits for the UROBs.*

Think of core pursuits as "hobbies on steroids." Taking trips, making art, exploring ancient ruins, building model ships, restoring old cars, blowing glass, writing novels, penning poetry, doing taxidermy—there are as many choices as there are happy retirees to pursue them. We'll take an expanded look at core pursuits in Chapter 4, where I will urge you to travel, play, and explore.

It follows, then, that vacations are vitally important. Happy retirees take 2.4 vacations a year versus 1.4 for the less happy. You may be thinking to yourself, "That's just a difference of one vacation!" But from my research, that one vacation may have made all the difference between being happy and being miserable.

HROBs love lakes, mountains, and oceans. They don't really discriminate. What they do like is to get away. And while we're at it, staycations don't count. Staycationers were 2.5 times more likely to land in the unhappy camp.

The happiest retirees maintain *a sense of awe and wonder about the world*. They have a thirst for progress and learning that can only be quenched with an adventurous spirit. In the infamous words of the late great Anthony Bourdain, "If I'm an advocate for anything, it's to move. As far as you can, as much as you can. Across the ocean, or simply across the river. Walk in someone else's shoes or at least eat their food. It's a plus for everybody."[4]

My data also revealed that *retirees who live "near or close" to at least half of their children or more see skyrocketing happiness levels compared with those who don't.* Maybe you're raising an eyebrow, thinking, "Being close to family is supposed to keep me happy?" I see you; I hear you. After all, I have a teenager! But like it or not, my research found that the happiest families are close, figuratively and literally—just not *too* close.

HROBs had *adult children who were financially independent and living out in the world*, whereas UROBs were more likely to have adult children still living at home, unable to leave the nest. You'll want to check out Chapter 5 for a more in-depth discussion on maintaining healthy relationships with family members during retirement, without watching them sap all your happiness away.

What about love and marriage? My research gave invaluable insight into that, too, including some results that were surprising. If you're wondering whether or not you can get a divorce and still be happy, my advice might go against the grain. But the numbers don't lie, and the numbers are clear: *you only get one (divorce, that is)*.

I also looked at different phases of marriage and tabulated happiness levels accordingly—and made some fascinating discoveries (Figure 1.1). You'll find the dirty deets on different marriage timelines in Chapter 6, but for all you true romantics: when couples have weathered the ups and downs of marriage for over 40 years, their happiness skyrockets. At 40+ years, *couples are two times happier than at any other point in their marriage* besides their honeymoon. I call this the "We made it!" phase.

Of course, you don't have to be a hopeless romantic to be happy in retirement, beholden to heart-eye emojis and two glasses of champagne (though if you want to live longer, you should absolutely drink champagne).[5] Friendships are just as important— if not *more* important—than marriages. *Happy retirees are experts at cultivating their social support systems.* In Chapter 8, we'll see that HROBs are social creatures; they know deep in their bones that they have to stay connected to stay happy. (Bones that, by the way, probably have lower rates of osteoporosis because happy retirees eat right and exercise regularly.)

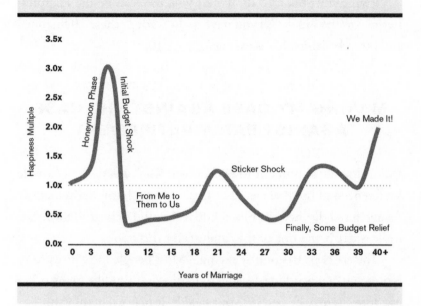

FIGURE 1.1 **Happiness on the Journey Through Marriage**

It goes without saying that we can't talk about happiness without talking about health. Anyone who has ever been sick for an extended period of time knows that without good health, not much else matters. That's why *the happiest retirees are active*. Period. They love what I call the "*ings*"—walking, hiking, biking, running, jogging, swimming. Golf and tennis are popular, a way to marry being social with staying fit. Tennis is my particular favorite. Time to dust off that backhand!

In Chapter 9, we'll have a heart-to-heart about health, exercise, diet, and alcohol in relation to retirement happiness. If you're jonesing for a nip of the strong stuff, I've got good news: alcohol may get a bad rap, but I give you full permission to imbibe. My studies showed that *happy retirees love to drink white wine and gin*. So next time you pick up a bottle, raise a glass for me.

I wrote this book to show that you, too, can be the Happiest Retiree on the Block. All you have to do is adopt these 10 financial and lifestyle habits. It's as easy as 1, 2 . . . 10.

MAKING MY CASE AGAINST THE CASE AGAINST EARLY RETIREMENT

I want to take a moment to address the *Wall Street Journal* article I referenced in the Preface, "The Case Against Early Retirement."[6] As much as I disliked the piece, I do feel a kind of begrudging gratitude, since it was one of the catalysts for this book.

The article starts out by saying, "Most people look forward to retirement, a reward for decades of hard work. But like many other pleasures, it may be bad for your health. It may even kill you."

Right out of the gate, that rubbed me the wrong way. For one thing, the wording doesn't sit right with me. I believe retirement is a privilege that you attain with great pride. It's not a "pleasure." It's not a recreational drug. It's a crucial life decision.

Then there's the crux of the writer's—in my opinion—flawed argument. Multiple studies from around the world show it's very easy and even probable to fall into a trap of inactivity after retirement, the consequence of a sedentary lifestyle and lack of socialization. For me, that pitfall is really indicative of a lack of purpose, which often goes hand in hand with a lack of curiosity. Combined, those *do* lead to increased rates of mortality. No objection there.

My issue is that the *Journal* published these findings under the veneer of an anti–early retirement screed. They chose a clickbait headline, one that implied people shouldn't retire early, when in fact the article itself was saying something far less incendiary: that if you don't do it right, it can be dangerous.

I couldn't agree more. My goal is to show you the *right* way to retire sooner, by adopting the right financial and lifestyle habits. But unlike my friends at the *WSJ*, I just don't think you have to keep working to do any of those things.

The article does, however, reference a study that's very interesting. In 2018, Cornell University and the University of Melbourne used administrative data covering the entire US adult population to examine how mortality rates change at age 62, which is when Americans can begin collecting Social Security retirement benefits. There was a statistically significant uptick in the mortality rate for men at 62. "After all," says the author, cheekily, "death is the definitive indicator of poor physical health, which itself is difficult to measure."

What is it about 62? Why do people at that specific age run into so much trouble? The researchers at Cornell and Melbourne concluded that the numbers were driven largely by increases in deaths from lung cancer and chronic obstructive pulmonary disease. It stands to reason that, once retired, these men smoked more and/or reduced their physical activity—behaviors that contribute to these types of deaths.

I would go even further. At 62, when these men first start collecting Social Security, they are going through a huge mental and emotional shift. More often than not, their social networks shrink as they interact with others less frequently. If they haven't cultivated any core pursuits, they're left with a lot of time and no way to fill it. They're listless, sedentary, bored. Since they're not being active, their physical health declines. Their mental health follows suit. They don't feel satisfied or fulfilled, and the downward spiral continues.

Consider the results from a recent study out of the Netherlands, analyzed by the Center for Retirement Research at Boston

College.[7] The researchers studied men and women who were financially encouraged to work an extra three years, and then isolated data from a five-year period to explore how the policy impacted mortality. The result? The five-year mortality risk for men in their early sixties dropped by an incredible 32 percent while the incentive program was in effect. Those three extra years increased their longevity, clear evidence that human beings are meant to be pursuing something, with purpose, until the very end of their lives.

"But, Wes," you say. "Don't these surveys undermine your point of view? If we live longer by working three extra years, why do you want a million people to retire early? Are you *trying* to kill us?"

Short answer: no. Long answer: I interpret the data from these studies very differently than my nemesis at the *Journal*. In my opinion, this study demonstrates the power of a sense of purpose, accomplishment, curiosity, and adventure. These are some of the best medicines available to combat the decline that can come with aging. You can scour this book from cover to cover, and you will never find me suggesting that a happy retirement is one in which you sit back, smoke a cigarette, and do nothing.

But the idea that going to work is our best shot at feeling a sense of purpose, accomplishment, curiosity, and adventure? It's simply not true. At least not for the vast majority of Americans. And the data backs me up. Here's an alarming statistic I cribbed from a Gallup poll a few years back: only about one in five Americans are fully engaged in their work.[8] These folks love their work and feel a sense of purpose from their jobs. Lucky them! Another three in five Americans have a "take it or leave it" attitude when it comes to their work. It may give them satisfaction and a sense of achievement from time to time, but it doesn't light them up inside—and they definitely don't want to be doing it forever.

The remaining one in five?

They hate their jobs so much they actively want to bring their employers down. That's 20 percent of Americans quietly working to undermine their companies! There is a reason that my most popular video on YouTube is "5 Reasons to Retire as Soon as You Can." One of those reasons is a boss from hell. Another is being underappreciated at your job.

And that, my friends, is why it's so exciting for me to launch this project. I want to liberate you from the job you either hate or feel "meh" about. For me, that means two things: helping you retire early *and* helping you retire *well*. It's not just about the quantity of those years you're getting back; it's the quality.

That's why I wrote this book. It's right there in the subtitle, the thread stitching all the financial and lifestyle habits together. I want to help you craft a life that's healthy, secure, and joyful. Now *that's* a retirement worth living.

Before we delve into the simple, actionable, life-changing habits that can transform your retirement, let's take a trip to the dark side.

In other words, the UROB side of the street.

CHAPTER 2

Who Is Your Unhappy Neighbor?

Have you seen *The Great Outdoors*?

If not, I highly recommend it. It's a tragically underrated movie from 1988, written by John Hughes, the famed writer and director of *Sixteen Candles*, *The Breakfast Club*, and *Weird Science*.

The basic plot goes like this: a lovable father's cherished family vacation in the woods is upended when his in-laws arrive uninvited. John Candy plays Chet, the lovable father. The dreaded in-laws are led by their patriarch, Uncle Roman, played beautifully by Dan Aykroyd.

Uncle Roman just might be the best UROB (Unhappiest Retiree on the Block) who's ever UROB'd.

Of course, when I first saw the movie, I didn't know that yet.

In Chapter 1, we met Ron and Rita Margarita, prime examples of the Happiest Retirees on the Block. We took a bird's-eye view of the financial and lifestyle habits that HROBs keep—habits you, too, can adopt to safeguard your retirement happiness.

In this chapter, we're going to meet some UROBs. We'll investigate the money choices and decisions they've made—and the bad habits they've picked up—that landed them solidly in the unhappy camp. I believe only by looking your enemy dead in the eyes can you know how best to defeat him.

So, without further ado: Uncle Roman.

CHET RIPLEY AND THE PLATEAU EFFECT

In *The Great Outdoors*, Uncle Roman is a big-time corporate executive. He's the kind of guy who loves talking about work, complaining about work, and counting his chips.

Most of us have known an Uncle Roman. He's the one who's always richer than you—or so he wants you to believe. He always finds a way to mention his luxury car (probably a BMW), his vacation home, his hot stock tips, and work work work.

At the start of the movie, Uncle Roman's wealth and success are undeniable. Our first glimpse of him isn't even of him, it's of his fancy car speeding along a mountain road. His license plate reads "ROMAN 1." I don't have the stats to back this up—I'll have to commission a new survey—but my guess is that a majority of HROBs don't feel a strong urge to purchase vanity license plates. It betrays a certain insecurity that happy retirees simply don't have.

The first time we actually see Uncle Roman out of the car, the camera lingers on his expensive ring and gold watch. We're only allowed to see his face *after* his glitzy possessions. We get the feeling the camera is obeying Roman's own PR strategy—precious metals maketh the man.

Spoiler alert: in the end, Uncle Roman isn't as rich as he first appears, which is true for more UROBs than you'd think. Let's just say that he let his Rich Ratio get way out of whack. Put a pin in that one—we'll come back to it later.

When sitting with the humble Chet on the porch overlooking beautiful Lake Potowotominimac, Uncle Roman is unable to appreciate the beauty of nature.

"I'll tell you what I see when I look out there. . . . I see the undeveloped resources of northern Minnesota, Wisconsin, and Michigan. I see a syndicated development consortium exploiting over a billion and a half dollars in forest products. I see a paper mill, and . . . a greenbelt between the condos on the lake and a waste management facility focusing on the newest rage in toxic waste, medical refuse. Infected bandages, body parts, IV tubing, contaminated glassware, entrails, syringes, fluids, blood, low grade radioactive waste, all safely contained, sunken in the lake, and sealed for centuries."

Chet, bewildered, responds that he only sees "trees." Uncle Roman lobs a smug insult, "Well, maybe it's all for the best. While the ambitious scramble for wealth and power, the Chet Ripleys of the world are just able to lay back and casually stroll along life's path"—but then something interesting happens.

"I mean that as a compliment," Uncle Roman admits. "The rest of us are all probably going to die of heart attacks and strokes long before ya."

Roman laughs, effectively ruining the moment. But over the course of the movie, we start to see more of his humanity, including the regret he feels about his life choices. In a later scene, Uncle Roman asks his wife: "Why is it that Chet's kids look at him like he's Zeus and my kids look at me like I'm a rack of yard tools at Sears?" He's headed toward a life as a UROB, and he can sense it, even if on a subconscious level.

Yet when Uncle Roman's wife tries to respond with helpful advice about connecting more with his kids by spending less time at work, he interrupts her to take a business call on a hilariously large

1980s cell phone. "Put a cork in it, honey. Talkin' business." Uncle Roman can't get out of his own way.

That's how it is with UROBs. Even when vacationing in a mountain cabin, they miss the forest for the trees.

As the movie progresses, it becomes more and more clear that Chet, not Uncle Roman, is the lucky one. Even before we realize Uncle Roman has far less money than he pretends to (read: he's broke), we see how unnecessary and unhealthy his priorities are.

Chet may not have a million-dollar stock portfolio, but he has enough savings to take his family on a nice vacation. He has enough money to enjoy life and do the things that are important to him, his wife, and his kids.

You may have heard me talk about the Plateau Effect of money and happiness.[1] No matter what the TV pundits tell you, you don't need millions upon millions to be happy. At a certain monetary inflection point, happiness levels don't keep inflating, even if the Benjamins do. Economists call this "diminishing marginal returns," suggesting that each incremental dollar past a certain point buys less and less. In this case, the diminishing marginal returns are on our happiness. I call it the Plateau Effect.

The Plateau Effect was one of my earliest inspirations for writing *You Can Retire Sooner Than You Think*. In the Preface I talked about how, in 2010, I read about the Princeton University study that showed happiness leveled off once people reached an income in the neighborhood of $75,000 per year.[2] In other words: happiness *can* correlate to having more money, but the graph doesn't look like Mount Everest. It looks more like if you chopped the peak off Mount Everest and then sanded it down flat and built a giant deck on top. Wouldn't it be cool to sit on a deck on Mt. Everest and sip some top-shelf Hendrick's gin? It's a weird visual, but you get the idea. Happiness levels don't continue to rise exponentially in relation to the amount of money you have. They—wait for it—*plateau*.

What the Plateau Effect teaches us is that we don't need endless money. My research has shown over and over that happiness, well-being, and security *relative to money* tend to level off. Yes, we need to get to a certain point, whether we're talking about active income or savings. But after that point, will gobs of money make us gobs happier? No.

Let's go back to Chet Ripley, happily barbecuing hot dogs on that deck we placed on top of a flattened Mount Everest. Meanwhile, Uncle Roman is at base camp, chasing the kind of salary it would take to barbecue lobster tails.

Don't be an Uncle Roman. Be a Chet.

J. PAUL GETTY, MISERABLE MISER MILLIONAIRE

My favorite real-life UROB was the legendary millionaire J. Paul Getty. He made Uncle Roman look like Father of the Year.

In 1966, the *Guinness Book of Records* named J. Paul Getty the world's richest private citizen, worth an estimated $1.2 billion. As famous as he was for amassing wealth in the oil industry and for his jaw-dropping art collection—he owned paintings by Titian, Renoir, Degas, and Monet, to name a few—J. Paul Getty is perhaps more famous for being the kind of miserable bastard who would refuse to shell out a pittance of his wealth to rescue his own kidnapped grandson.

Imagine you have $1.2 billion in cash and assets. One day your 16-year-old grandson is kidnapped by an Italian organized-crime syndicate. Would you be willing to part with $17 million to ensure his safe return?

J. Paul Getty was not. In fact, not until after the kidnappers cut off his grandson's ear and sent it to a newspaper did Mr. Getty agree to pay any kind of ransom. Even then, he refused to pay a penny over $2.2 million—the maximum amount that was tax deductible—and lent the remainder to his son, who was responsible for repaying the sum at 4 percent interest. Imagine doing your taxes and trying to deduct the "grandson ransom" line item. I'm not sure H&R Block has a form for that.

I use the story of J. Paul Getty as a cautionary tale. Happiness in retirement is not just about money. It's also not about how much oil you sell or your quarterly earnings report. It's about where you put your priorities, what you're curious about, and the stuff you love.

In my opinion, J. Paul Getty's actions revealed a love for money and status far more than a love for life. Just because his estate was big enough to be the only house on the block, doesn't mean he wasn't the unhappiest one on it.

THE MYSTERIOUS MR. MORCOTT

Now that I've introduced you to two depressing examples of UROBs, it's time for a change of scenery.

I'm lucky enough to have spent some time up in Harbor Springs, Michigan. It's a quaint and beautiful town situated right by the clear water of Little Traverse Bay. The houses on the water sell for ungodly sums—$10 million plus—but if you're living in the town proper, it's actually somewhat affordable. In the summer you can boat on the bay, and in the winter you can ski at the nearby Boyne Highlands and Nub's Nob Ski Resort.

It's safe to say Harbor Springs is one of my favorite places in the world. Last time I was there, I became friendly with a neighbor who simply referred to himself as "Woody." We bonded over the fact that both our wives are nurses. He told me about his grown children, and I introduced him to my little ones.

Woody was probably in his late seventies and seemed like a really happy guy. An avid golfer, at one point he had a small house in Scotland, the birthplace of the sport. He delighted me with tales of golf swings, golf buddies, and golf courses. I'm not sure what his handicap was on the links, but whenever we teed off, laughter was par for the course.

Two days after we met, I woke up to an issue of *Golf Digest: Northern Michigan* on my front doorstep, with the corner folded on a page titled *Top 10 Places to Play Within 50 Miles*. His favorites were highlighted. "You should try here with the boys," read a thoughtful note attached. From dogleg holes to dog-eared pages, Woody knew how to drive it straight down the fairway. I only wish he could have helped me with my swing.

It wasn't until the end of the first week that Woody's career even came up. As we were discussing all things Michigan, he commented that it used to be the car company guys who would come up and buy vacation homes, the executives from the Big Three automobile companies: Chrysler, Ford, and GM. In recent years, he told me, the companies had struggled, and fewer and fewer execs had been coming up to purchase second homes.

At this point, I decided to find out more about Woody's life.

"What did you do?" I asked.

"I was in the car business," he said with a shrug, and left it at that.

Well, I looked into it later that night. Turns out his career summary was a bit of an understatement. A quick Google search revealed he was the former CEO and chairman of Dana Corporation, Southwood J. "Woody" Morcott. At the time of his retirement, he had nearly 30 years of service to the company, with the last 10 as chairman.

Woody was clearly a mogul in the car business, a well-respected industry legend with a long, storied career. But what struck me the most was that I had been talking to him for an entire week and it never even came up.

Why? Because Woody wanted to talk about his grandkids down in Florida, the top five golf courses he'd played, and the fact that he couldn't wait to play in Scotland again someday.

Ladies and gentlemen, *that* is a happy retiree. A pure-grade HROB, no doubt about it.

Woody had a wildly successful career and made a lot of money along the way. Do I want that for you? Yes! But if you think that's all it's about, you're missing the point. The entire time he was climbing the corporate ladder, he was also bringing his kids up to Northern Michigan. He was wiping snotty noses and baiting fishing hooks. He was making Saturday morning pancakes. He was daydreaming about life outside of work and what he really wanted to do. And now he's reaping the benefits of that curiosity, connectedness, and financial foresight.

Was Woody passionate about his job? Absolutely. You don't become a CEO without a strong drive. But your high school quarterback was passionate about his job, too. Unless he found something deeper—or his name was Tom Brady—his life peaked prematurely. The HROBs don't do that. They keep throwing touchdowns long after the game ends.

To this day, two of Woody's three kids live near him when he's back home in Florida. He loves life. The great Woody Morcott. He was only on my block for a few weeks, but there was no doubt he was the happiest one on it.

In my role as a managing partner at Capital Investment Advisors, I've met a lot of unhappy folks. Some were entrepreneurs who worked 24/7 for 30 years and literally didn't know how to stop. What's the point of retirement if you have no interest in or curiosity about anything else? Golf, tennis, walking, hiking, biking—

it's all boring and unproductive to this type of UROB. He or she never "has the time," even when staring at a blank social calendar.

Some of the UROBs I've met are "pretend rich" like Uncle Roman, and some are legitimately rich like J. Paul Getty. Most have allowed work to define them, rather than actually living their lives like HROBs do. Now, in retirement, they're reaping the compound interest of 20, 30, 40 years of accumulated bad habits. That's not the kind of interest anyone wants.

Maybe you're thinking, "How do I know if I'm on the path to becoming a UROB, Wes? What if it's too late for me?"

The good news is that it's never too late. I work with pre-retirees, yes, but I also work with people already in retirement who have realized the error of their ways.

Emphasis on *realized*. Because if you feel yourself veering toward unhappiness, the first step is always awareness.

YOU MIGHT BE AN UNHAPPY RETIREE IF . . .

I'll try to make this as painless as possible. Think of it like Jeff Foxworthy's standup routine. Jeff always starts his set with: "You might be a redneck if . . ."

1. You Might Be a UROB If You Drive a BMW

This survey result was one of the most hotly debated parts of *You Can Retire Sooner Than You Think*. Controversial for BMW lovers? Sure. But the statistics don't lie.

My research showed that the number one luxury brand for unhappy retirees was BMW. I guess I shouldn't be surprised that to date no BMW dealerships have offered to endorse my books.

But *why* do UROBs drive BMWs? I've had a lot of time to ponder this. I'll tell you what I think: there's something about the performance-oriented, fine-cutting, hard-driving, expensive-to-repair flashiness of a BMW that leads to unhappiness in retirement.

I don't know any other way to describe it. To this day, when I look at a BMW, it just screams: *I'm trying to prove something!* To whom? To my friends? To my spouse? To myself? Maybe all of the above. To me, it connotes a level of insecurity in the driver, suggesting there's a gap he or she is trying to fill. Rather than finding an organic, self-reflective, and healthy way to do it, the person is deflecting these feelings of inadequacy onto "The Ultimate Driving Machine."

Ironically, a BMW isn't even the most expensive car on the luxury list. Plenty of other lavish vehicles tip the money scales. So if it isn't money that leads unhappy retirees to pick BMW, what is it?

It's money's first cousin: monetary status.

Something HROBs understand is that it doesn't pay to place any value on monetary status. When advertisers try to sell you on the idea that specific goods and services will bring you happiness, they're selling you false hope. Happy retirees know this. Unhappy ones don't.

For whatever reason—pop culture, movies, music videos—BMWs have an enduring level of status. I blame the (admittedly) great 1996 film *Clueless*, starring Alicia Silverstone and Paul Rudd. Alicia's character, Cher, is rich and beautiful. Her equally rich and beautiful best friend, Dionne, drives around in a red convertible 325i Cabrio BMW because that's exactly what audiences would expect a rich and beautiful person to drive.

Monetary status is baked into the sticker price of a BMW. The key for happy retirees is not to need that status. The BMW might do 0 to 60 in 4.6 seconds, but not without leaking your happiness engine dry.

The happiest retirees don't need the flashiest luxury brand, but they still want to enjoy the ride. Think Lexus. Think Acura, Buick, or Toyota. Leave the BMW on the lot.

2. You Might Be a UROB If You're Too Keyed Up About Investments

The obsessing-over-money thing is not good. Trust me. I've seen it many times. There is a big difference between being actively involved in your investment portfolio and taking on a second career as a stock trader.

For one thing: that's not the point of retirement. Never in all my years as an investment professional has a client said to me, "Wes, I can't wait to retire, so I can focus all my time and energy on chasing stocks!"

Don't get me wrong. It's a good idea to spend time with your finances, and you certainly want to have at least a base level of financial literacy. But once you get too far into the weeds, it's a red flag. Tormenting yourself over fast-moving facts and figures almost always leads to poor investment returns over time, not to mention the ongoing emotional toll and burden. Being glued to every drop or rise in the Dow Jones Industrial Average while you're in retirement? That's not making you more money. It's a formula for anxiety because investing is a bumpy, unpredictable game in the short term. Compulsion won't guarantee you returns, but it *will* guarantee that you drive yourself crazy. Obsession is not your friend.

I've seen this lead to unhappiness in retirement more than I care to admit. I've even had to let go clients over it. You read correctly: I have actively turned down business because the misery of my clients was rubbing off on me.

I remember one specific individual, a retired plaintiff attorney, who texted me every single night at 11 p.m. Whenever the market was down more than 5 percent, he went into full freak-out mode. "Here are some CNBC headlines, Wes. What are we gonna do? What's gonna happen? Where do we go from here?"

I was on edge each time I got a ping from him. He wanted to talk every single day, over and over and over again, about the problem du jour. He made every molehill into a mountain and wore us *both* out. We didn't work together long.

Financial planning doesn't need to last hours on end every single day. It needs to take an hour or two every weekend. Four or five hours a month—or even every quarter—goes a long way. Understanding your overarching goals, getting your budget in order, and understanding where you're invested is enough for most HROBs.

Besides, why would you want to volley finances back and forth with your spouse over and over again when you could be volleying tennis balls on a nice, sunny day? Go enjoy this person you've chosen to spend your life with. You finally have time!

3. You Might Be a UROB If You Live Far Away from More Than 50 Percent of Your Children

What do I mean by far away? Anything you can't reasonably drive to. A two-hour drive is fine. Three roadside hotels and 5 tanks of gas? Not so much.

Of the nearly 2,000 retirees I surveyed, the retirees who lived near at least half their children were two to five times more likely to be happy than those who did not.[3] Take a look at the chart in Figure 2.1. This shows the relationship between retirement happiness and the percentage of children who live close by. If Jim and

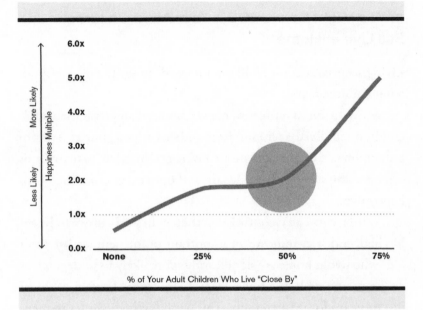

FIGURE 2.1 **Live Near the Kids**

Cara have four kids and live in Atlanta, they are five times more likely to be happy if three of those kids live in Georgia.

The happiest retirees say it's impossible to put a price tag on life experiences, especially memories made with children and grandchildren. Often, proximity to children isn't just about the parent-child relationship, but about being able to be good grandparents. An overwhelming amount of research is devoted to parent-child dynamics, yet, as other research shows, close grandparent-grandchild relationships are themselves a marker of strong family ties and come with their own distinctive benefits to well-being.[4]

Guess who lives close to two of his three children? Woody Morcott. Enough said.

4. You Might Be a UROB If Your Adult Children Still Live at Home

Living near your adult children is a good thing. Living *with* your adult children is not.

My data found retirees were two times *un*happier if their adult children still lived at home. Respondents noted similar levels of unhappiness if their adult children were not married, as marriage is often a catalyst for getting kids up and out and crafting their own happy lives.

While you can't control whether your kids ultimately get hitched, statistics indicate an important point: Unmarried adult kids who live at home are significantly more likely to be dependent on mom and dad. The financial and emotional burden of this is just too hard for many retirees. This period of life requires tremendous adjustment: careers, relationships, financial planning—all of these are in flux. Parents may struggle with how to appropriately care for or relate to a child who has become an adult but still resides in their home. They may also find themselves resenting the unexpected extension of parental responsibility in a season that was supposed to be "about them." Which leads me to:

5. You Might Be a UROB If Your Kids Are on Your Payroll

I've written in the past about the importance of moving adult kids toward independence.[5] While every child-retiree relationship is complex, every circumstance different, and every financial situation unique, the data shows that taking kids off the payroll—or at least giving them a pay cut—also boosts happiness in retirement.

Unhappy families average $714 a month in support of their twenty-, thirty-, and fortysomething-year-old "kids." Happy retirees spend less than $500 a month on their adult children. If your children are not financially independent, you are 1.5 times more likely to be an unhappy retiree. Think about it. If a happy retiree is living on $5,000 or $6,000 per month, $700 is a lot, right? That means 10 to 15 percent of your budget is going to your kids instead of fueling the next chapter of your life.

My study found that over 40 percent of retirees are giving their adult children some level of financial support. This doesn't include children with special needs or the occasional gift of a trip to Disneyland or Christmas cash. It means support from parents to subsidize everyday life. I'm talking about private schools for grandchildren, car leases, rent, mortgages, paying down debt, and more—because the kids can't afford the lifestyle they keep.

I'm not saying you're a bad person for helping your kids out. Heck, almost half of American retirees do it! The problem is that your generosity can have, at best, a negative impact, and at worst, a devastating effect on your own finances and happiness levels.

To take this to an extreme: a family supporting adult children with over $2,000 a month are more than four times more likely to be unhappy than a family with fully financially independent kids. That's quite a price tag.

This problem isn't going away anytime soon. A CNN article from September 2020 showed that 52 percent of young adults in the United States are living with their parents.[6] Blame whatever you want—the economy, Covid-19, TikTok—but you can't argue with facts: 52 percent is the highest that percentage has been since the Great Depression. This is a double-edged sword. We want to have our family close, as we've learned from HROBs. But overspending on our adult kids for BMW payments and private schools for grandchildren can weigh heavily, create resentment, and lead to higher levels of unhappiness.

The next time little Johnny and little Suzy ask for money to help pay for private school, maybe the answer should be, "Actually, we're going to spend that money going to Paris. We've got some traveling to make up for because of all those years we spent our extra money raising you and your siblings."

6. You Might Be a UROB If You've Been Divorced Twice or More

HROBs get one marriage redo. More than that, and you're more likely to be unhappy. Marital status is a critical variable of retirement happiness. If retirees are not married or have never been married, they are 4.5 times more likely to be unhappy. Happiness levels rise when you've been married one or two times. Beyond that, if you increase the number of times you have been married, you're asking for trouble—and I don't just mean from your ex.

7. You Might Be a UROB If You Had Two or Fewer Core Pursuits Before You Retired

If the happiest retirees I know are the most curious retirees, it is likewise true that the unhappiest retirees I know are the most *in*curious. They say curiosity killed the cat, but I think in retirement, it's the opposite. A lack of curiosity about new pursuits and passions can lead to an uninteresting, uninspiring, dull, and less purposeful life.

In other words: the domain of the UROB.

It's difficult to develop and start focusing on core pursuits that didn't exist before retirement. Just like saving money, you want to start nurturing your passions early. We all know there's a compounding effect when it comes to saving money. It's easier for us to accumulate higher levels of wealth if we start earlier. The same math applies to developing core pursuits.

It's tough to start playing golf at age 60. It's really tough to start playing tennis at age 70. It's almost impossible to become social when you're 80. If you've been out of shape and never exercised a day in your life, do you think it will be easy to flip a switch and run a marathon in retirement? Even more importantly, if you haven't forged an authentic and loving bond with your kids, why do you think you'll suddenly be able to do it later?

Unfortunately, many busy executives, high-level consultants, and small-business owners in America exhibit a singular obsession with their careers and fail to find time for core pursuits. Whether they own an engineering firm, advertising group, or home-building operation, it doesn't really matter—this is industry agnostic. These people run the risk of spending so much time and energy on their business that they forget why they're doing it and how they want to reap the rewards.

Full disclosure: I'm on this growth journey, too. I do love my career and my company, and I'm somewhat guilty of working well beyond the 60-hours-per-week mark. However, I've learned not to make it my life, my living, and my core pursuit all wrapped into one.

People who do this are frequently burned out. They push everything off to the future, rather than planning now for what they want to do later. "Once I sell, I'll pick up golf." No. Pick up golf now, even if you can't play as often as you want.

"Once I sell, I'll spend more time with my family." Wrong. Your family is so much more important. Look for ways to spend time with them now. Build those bonds. It will pay off later, once you have more time.

If your core pursuit ends up making you a little extra money? All the better. Look at Elon Musk. On the way to building a net worth of $100 billion plus, he also managed to "throw in" a core pursuit: his interest in space and space travel. As of mid-2021, SpaceX, his private company and pet project to colonize Mars, is worth more than $70 billion. Bonus perk: there's currently a Tesla Roadster freewheeling through space, millions of miles from Earth (seriously).

We can't all juice our core pursuits for billions. I'm not sure I'd want to. Just don't plan so hard for the future that you forget to create one.

Here's the deal: I know a lot of UROBs. I certainly have a few not-so-happy rich families I counsel. Older guys who still talk about work every day. They don't travel. They don't exercise. They're not social. They're like J. Paul Getty, but with 2 mansions instead of 20. Despite being in their mid-seventies, they're so focused on their career, it's as if they're talking about their high school football team. The Al Bundy Effect. Does anyone remember Al Bundy from *Married . . . with Children*? Or did I watch too much TV in the 1990s?

These guys aren't happy. No UROB is. Though they all have unique circumstances and situations, at the root of their unhappiness you'll find the same bad habits, lack of core pursuits, obsession over money, and adult kids who are overly dependent on them financially, or live too far away.

Every block is going to have an unhappy person. I don't want it to be you.

When it comes to money? Don't let it dominate your life. There's nothing intrinsically wrong with money—we all need it to survive. Make it, save it, spend it. But if you want to be the Happiest Retiree on the Block, you must see money as a means to an end, not the end itself. You must make your money work for you, not the other way around.

How do you do that?

By learning good money habits. Which is exactly what Chapter 3 is all about.

CHAPTER 3

Money Habits

THINK RIVER, NOT RESERVOIR

Last summer, my wife, four boys, dog, and I piled into one of those extended SUVs for our annual summer vacation. It takes 12 hours to drive from Atlanta to Ann Arbor where Lynne's parents live, which is where we always spend the night. From there it's another four hours to get to Harbor Springs in Northern Michigan.

If you've never taken a 16-hour road trip with four kids and a giant 110-pound red Labrador retriever, let me paint you a picture.

I was driving and Lynne was riding shotgun as the copilot, navigator, and backseat referee. Samuel, my youngest, was still in his car seat. My oldest, Ben, was in a regular seat, with Kodie the dog in the middle back, and Luke and Jake in the far back. We had a ton of luggage, four bikes, and a cargo carrier packed to bursting on the roof. Everyone was struggling for seats and space, just trying to survive what even in modern times felt like an eternity in the car.

The reality is that the kids were all on their devices, glued to their screens. But even with all the technology in the world, we ended up having family conversations, intercut with "I want KFC" and "*No*, I want McDonald's" and "*No*, I want Chick-fil-A."

On this particular road trip, we had a great conversation about turtles.

The boys were watching the latest *Teenage Mutant Ninja Turtles* on their iPad—actually a good movie—when I said, "Guys, did you know that in real life, Galapagos tortoises don't age? They have the same life expectancy at age 10 as they do at age 50 and 100."

I only knew this because I had recently interviewed Dr. Andrew Steele for my Retire Sooner podcast. Steele is a biogerontologist and the author of *Ageless: The New Science of Getting Older Without Getting Old*.

My son Luke, wise to hyperbole at the ripe old age of 11, didn't buy it. "Whatever, Dad. There's no way turtles live forever."

"I'm not saying they live forever," I countered. "They do die—they can get caught in a boat propeller or die from an infected cut, and they're still susceptible to disease. But genetically, they don't age. Their life expectancy doesn't change."

I told them about the oldest Galapagos tortoise on record, Adwaita, who died in a Calcutta zoo in 2006. Adwaita was said to be 250 years old, first taken to India by British sailors during the reign of King George II.[1]

I was winning the boys over, I could tell.

"So how old is the oldest turtle today?" asked Jake.

"One hundred ninety years old. That means it's been alive since before the Civil War."

Even Luke looked impressed.

I wasn't going to subject my kids to the latest episode of my podcast—but I did share more of what Dr. Steele told me. He believes that aging is "the single most important scientific challenge of our time."[2] In his book, he talks about how Galapagos tortoises get old without getting elderly. In the scientific community they describe this as "negligible senescence" when an organism does not exhibit evidence of biological aging. The larger implication, of course, is that we two-legged humans might be able to master "biological immortality" and become ageless too.

It may sound like pie in the sky, but Dr. Steele isn't a quack: he's a respected biologist. And he's not alone. Scientists around the world are figuring out how to take the knowledge gleaned from tortoises and other unaging animal species to create a medical solution—not a fountain of youth, but a way to increase our life expectancy. Steele told me they're treating aging as a disease that could be helped, cured, or slowed down. Maybe we'll be able to live one year longer. Maybe five. Maybe 20. We don't know. But it's in the works.

Here's my question for you. If you live 1, 5, or 20 years longer: how are you going to make your money last?

Let's say that, over the next few years, the biogeneticists get their way. Dr. Steele and his fellow scientists harness the age-defying potential of the Galapagos tortoises, and suddenly, if you take the right supplements—and assuming you steer clear of boat propellers—you can tack on an extra 10 years to your projected life span. Congratulations! That's 10 more years of being the Happiest Retiree on the Block.

The trick, of course, is figuring out the money side of the equation. If you're reading this book at 40 and live to be 115, will your money last as long as you do? And I don't mean just surviving: I want you to *thrive*. Even 65 is a super young retiree if you're going to live 50 more years. I want to make sure you have enough to live your best, fullest, longest, most purposeful life.

Will you live to be over 100? I certainly hope so. I'm not qualified to read your future—I deal in investment portfolios, not crystal balls. What I *am* qualified to tell you is that there are certain principles to follow before and during retirement to ensure your money lasts.

In the chapters that follow, we'll be delving into the engaging, empowering, enlightening habits of the happiest retirees. But first we have to lay the financial foundation for our HROB house—and it all starts with good money habits. In this chapter, I'm going to share with you the transformative money rules and strategies that unite the Happiest Retirees on the Block.

I've said it before, and I'll say it again: there are three core, actionable money habits that nearly all HROBs have in common. If you can check these off your retirement to-do list, you will be on your way to Happy Town, population: *you*.

The happiest retirees have:

1. **At least $500,000 in liquid retirement savings.** That's the inflection point for happiness: half a million. A net worth beyond $500,000 doesn't have nearly as much impact on higher happiness levels as getting to $500,000. Meaning, even as your savings continue to climb, your happiness won't necessarily rise at the same rate it did from zero to $500,000. Liquid retirement saving simply means that this is money you can access with ease, such as stocks, bonds, mutual funds, ETFs, cash, etc.

2. **A mortgage payoff that is complete or within sight.** This is a big one. We'll touch on it here, but a discussion of mortgages and other home-related habits takes center stage in Chapter 10.

3. **Multiple streams of retirement income.** It's right there in the chapter subtitle: think river, not reservoir. Actually, think *many* rivers. These tributaries will carry you away to retirement happiness.

In this chapter, we're going to dig a little deeper. We'll investigate the principles that go into each of these three money habits, including:

- Taxes, Savings, Life (TSL) Budgeting

- The One-Third Mortgage Payoff Rule

- The Rich Ratio

- Fill the Gap (FTG)

- The Retirement Grey Zone

Let's take a look at how to apply each of these rules and strategies—and why they matter for you.

$500,000 IN LIQUID RETIREMENT SAVINGS

Once a certain amount of wealth is attained, people experience diminishing marginal returns of happiness. As you already know, I've termed this phenomenon the Plateau Effect, and it's a key factor in determining how much money we need to be happy during retirement.

My research on happy retirees has yielded real and specific numbers to back up the Plateau Effect. In terms of liquid net worth (including stocks, bonds, mutual funds, and cash), retirees with around $100,000 reported feeling unhappy or just slightly happy.

Here's where it gets really interesting.

See how the line levels off at the top of the graph in Figure 3.1? Looking at median data on liquid net worth, the $100,000 mark was where folks were stuck in the not happy or only slightly happy

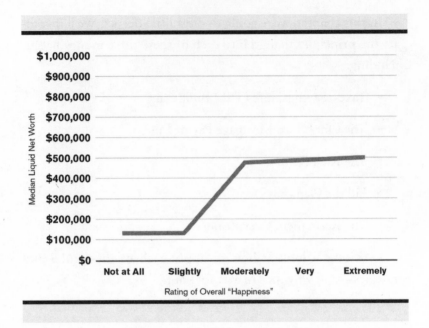

FIGURE 3.1 **Happiness by Median Liquid Net Worth**

zone. But once they hit $500,000, they moved decidedly into the moderately happy through extremely happy zone.

How did I reach this number? It's the product of both my professional experience and extensive research. The results of my survey made it crystal clear: with just a half-a-million-dollar nest egg, you can live a happy and financially secure retirement. While everyone's exact economic needs vary, this number can work for retirees who carry little debt and don't live an extravagant lifestyle. Instead of setting your sights sky-high for numbers like $2 million or $10 million, you should first aim for a healthy $500,000 in savings.

Of course, $500,000 may still sound like a lot of money, especially if you're a twenty- or thirtysomething who's still accumulating wealth. I'm not saying half a million is chump change. But it is a much more attainable goal than $2 million, and no matter your income level, you have a better chance of reaching it.

How? You start by budgeting.

I've always recommended a straightforward budgeting methodology where for three months you're very intentional about tracking your spending. If you are able to track it via a software program, fantastic. You can also manually add up your expenses at the end of every month using your credit card or bank statements.

The easiest budget program ever created is what I call my TSL (Taxes, Savings, Life) budgeting approach. In preretirement, approximately 30 percent of your income should be allocated for taxes, 20 percent for savings, and 50 percent for life (all the necessities and fun!).

Let's say you have 40 years to invest and build for your retirement. If you simply take $100 each month and invest it, assuming a 10 percent return and that your investment compounds monthly, you'll have a sweet $637,000 at the end of those four decades.

A 10 percent annual rate of return, you say? You may be surprised by the following. Despite three wicked bear market corrections over the past 20 years, the S&P has still averaged over 7 percent per year, including reinvested dividends.[3] During this time, REITs, a common option in most 401(k) plans, have averaged over 10 percent per year.[4] And over even longer periods of time, such as the past 40 years, the S&P 500 has averaged over 11 percent per year when dividends are included. I'm not saying these returns have been a given for most investors, nor is there a guarantee that this profitable run will continue forever. However, if you have a long time horizon, 20 years or more, then using a 10 percent assumption in this example is constructive.

So there you have it. The secret to a happy retirement isn't having $2 million in the bank, no matter what Suze Orman may tell you. On a recent podcast, Orman raised eyebrows with a bold statement about how much money people need to retire. "You need at least $5 million," she said, "or $6 million. Really, you might need $10 million."[5]

Really, Suze? A number like that cuts most people off at the knees before they even get started. Suze may want you to work forever, but I certainly don't.

Happiness in retirement is about having a simple plan, getting started, and being committed to having at least $500,000 saved up by the time you retire. The vast majority of the HROBs featured in this book do not have millions upon millions in retirement savings—and they were still able to stop working and live joyful, fulfilling lives.

A MORTGAGE PAYOFF THAT IS COMPLETE OR WITHIN SIGHT

I believe the happiest retirees enter post-career life either mortgage-free or within five years of hosting a mortgage-burning party. This insight comes from the extensive research I conducted for *You Can Retire Sooner Than You Think*.

The argument you'll hear from the camp of pro-mortgage pros is that you can do better by investing your savings as you continue to pay interest on your house. As an example, these planners say that, instead of using $100,000 to pay off a 4 percent mortgage, you should invest it in the market, where you could see a return of, say, 8 or 10 percent. The result: a net 4 to 6 percent gain.

Hmm. This logic looks good on paper, but it may not hold up as well in the real world. As we all know, the market can drop or stay flat for relatively extended periods of time, and our gains should be measured in decades, not years. And since the average life span of a mortgage in the United States due to frequent housing moves is *less* than 10 years, this timeline might not work.

I'm a believer in the One-Third Rule. If you can pay off your mortgage with no more than one-third of your *non*retirement savings accounts, you should consider doing so. For our purposes, nonretirement simply means after tax brokerage or savings accounts, not your 401(k), IRA, or retirement savings plans from work. If you owe $50,000 and have $160,000 in savings, drop that bomb on the mortgage. You will still have $110,000 in liquid assets to ease you along the retirement road.

In addition to financial considerations, think about how your mortgage affects your emotional health. I've learned from the happiest retirees that there is a real sense of peace and serenity that comes with knowing you own your house free and clear. It just feels good as you enter a new phase of life that is chock-full of changes.

Eliminating a house payment also dramatically lowers your monthly retirement living expenses, taking the pressure off your nest egg and other sources of monthly income. This step leaves you with more money to follow your dreams and passions—for travel, hobbies, or charitable giving. In other words: your core pursuits. That's what a happy retirement is all about.

But you must be sure that you can afford this peace of mind without putting undue strain on your financial fitness. It is rarely a good idea to use retirement-account money—IRA, 401(k)— to pay off a mortgage. Remember, paying off your mortgage is about creating peace of mind. Tapping your retirement nest egg too heavily too early might end up being counterproductive. Large withdrawals from an IRA or 401(k) to pay off a mortgage can dramatically raise your tax bracket and cost you more in taxes than if you were to spread out your mortgage payoff over time.

So if you can't dump a pile of money on your mortgage right now, consider paying a little extra each month. This way, you can shave months (or years) off the time that you'll be making payments. And you will be further on the road most traveled by the HROBs: living mortgage free.

MULTIPLE STREAMS OF RETIREMENT INCOME

For all you devoted readers of my first book: Do you remember Rich?

Rich Ratio, that is. We talked about the Rich Ratio in *You Can Retire Sooner Than You Think*, but here's a refresher: this is my system of making sure you are living below your means because that's the crux of wealth building. Put simply, the Rich Ratio is a straightforward way to measure the amount of money you have in relation to the amount of money you need.

Here's how to determine your Rich Ratio:

First, calculate your total monthly income. If you're still working and looking for the ratio you'll likely have during retirement, then use projected values. Remember to consider all possible retirement income streams: paychecks from part-time work, Social Security and/or pension benefits, rental income, miscellaneous sources, and, of course, the amount your investments should produce. Also, make sure to adjust this number for taxes so you have a "net income" number to work with.

Now that you have an income figure, it's time to calculate your needs. To do this, simply use your projected monthly retirement budget. With these two numbers, our equation looks like this:

$$\text{Have} \div \text{Need} = \text{Rich Ratio}$$

For the more visual folks out there, why we want a ratio of 1 or more may be clearer now. The reason is that we want what we have to be greater than what we need. In economics, supply and demand ratios fluctuate, but when it comes to being a happy retiree, what we have (supply) must always be greater than what we need (demand).

This system works regardless of your income level. A Rich Ratio greater than 1 is fantastic. A Rich Ratio under 1 means there is room for improvement. Let's say you generate $8,000 per month (after taxes) and you only need $4,000 to meet your obligations, giving you a Rich Ratio of 2. You're rich! If your monthly income is $1 million, but your spending needs are $2 million (Rich Ratio 0.5), then I'm sorry to report that you are poor.

HROBs have to figure out how to bring money in the door once they head into retirement. While it's nice to get a steady paycheck from an employer or to pay ourselves (as business owners), we have to change our mindset before we retire. When it comes to generating income, it's a good idea to go from relying on one income stream to many.

Essentially, you're creating as many tributaries as possible to come together in one new, predictable, larger river of income. You likely already have ideas about where you can gain other sources of income. These could include multiple pensions, Social Security, rental properties, investments, or part-time work.

Let's talk for a moment about part-time work. There are many retirees who may be ready to retire from a full-time career but are still interested in working at least part-time. In fact, an estimated one in five retirees continues to work in some capacity after leaving their full-time careers. If you're interested in working part-time to have an income stream in retirement, consider a job doing something you're passionate about. Maybe it's something completely unrelated to what you used to do. Or if you loved what you used to do, you might try consulting. While part-time work may be less income, be less secure, and include fewer benefits, it's a great way to bring in a supplemental paycheck once your main career comes to an end.

Maybe you were earning $250,000 a year and almost killing yourself in the process. Now you might decide you don't really need to save any more money, so you can stop putting money into that bucket. This could potentially mean downshifting from a $250,000 annual salary to a $50,000 salary, rather than stopping work entirely. You'll obviously earn less at this part-time job, sure, but on the plus side: your overall tax rate should fall dramatically.

Maybe you were a teacher or scientist, and now you can work from home a couple of days per week. Maybe you were a nurse like my wife, and you can choose to practice via telework instead. Maybe you're in the real estate industry—residential or commercial—and you can work from home now and only keep a handful of clients. Being an attorney is great for this sort of thing. Billable hours, baby!

There are so many ways to use your original skills in a much less demanding environment while still making enough money to avoid tapping much, or any, of your savings. Whatever your profession, find a way to make a smart, meaningful downshift. There are multiple methods to identify the gap in your income and take the right steps to fill it.

Which brings me to my next strategy.

FILL THE GAP

One of the biggest worries about retirement is that you won't have enough money set aside when the time comes. Knowledge is a powerful weapon for battling fear. The more we know about any challenge, the less scary it becomes.

Allow me to introduce my Fill the Gap (FTG) strategy, a simple but powerful way to understand how much money you need in retirement and how much your investments have to contribute to meet that need.

FTG consists of three simple steps:

1. **Figure out your post-retirement net income.** This part should be simple. Take all of your guaranteed income streams (from sources like Social Security and pensions) and add them up. Then deduct what you will likely owe in taxes. If you know you'll be getting $3,500 per month (after taxes), then this number is your "take-home income."

2. **Determine your monthly spending.** Tally up all of your monthly expenses. You may use Excel, Quicken, or just good old-fashioned pencil and paper. For this example, let's say your monthly expenses come out to $5,000 per month.

3. **Find your gap.** Subtract your take-home income from your spending needs. Here, we have: $5,000 – $3,500 = $1,500. That $1,500 figure is the perpetual gap you must fill. Remember that it will need to be adjusted over time for inflation and as your spending changes.

That gap will ideally be filled by your nest egg. According to the well-established 1,000-Bucks-a-Month Rule—really more of a rule of thumb—someone who retires at the typical age of 62 to 65 needs $240,000 in savings for every $1,000 a month they need to fill the gap.[6] (This assumes a 5 percent annual withdrawal rate.) So in the scenario above, the retiree would need $360,000 in savings to meet their monthly needs. ($1,500 × 12 months = $18,000/ year divided by 5% = $360,000)

There are nearly endless ways to approach investing for retirement. Growth, momentum, long-short, international, small cap, venture, private equity—the list goes on. I happen to be partial to a style called income investing, as is can help you get comfortable with how much your portfolio is generating in cash flow (not just growth) in any given year. On the income side, income investors can aim for at least 3 or 4 percent yield on client investments.

What exactly are we talking about here? Cash flow. Income. We are homing in on the dividends, interest, and distributions that investors can enjoy from income-oriented stocks, exchange-traded funds (ETFs), bonds, real estate investment trusts (REITs), and master limited partnerships (MLPs). Investors can often get to a 3, 4, or even 5 percent annual yield, which is the actual cash flow portion that is paid out to you or added to your account. Note that your cash flow should only be part of your overall total return equation

On the appreciation side, the situation is more fluid, as returns tend to fluctuate with the stock market and the overall economy's performance. As a rule of thumb, you should shoot for an annual gain (over time) of another 4 to 5 percent from this part of the equation.

Combine our two factors and, depending on your risk tolerance, you should be looking to achieve an overall annual percentage of somewhere in the 5.5 to 10.0 percent range. All things considered, I've found this to be a reasonable range, provided you have a long and patient time horizon, and the risk tolerance for asset fluctuation.

I want to restate the importance of using *after-tax dollars* in your FTG calculations. Retirees often see a dramatic drop in their overall effective tax rate once they stop working, so it pays to do some research into your projected tax rate.

For example, let's say you were used to seeing 30 to 35 percent of your paycheck go to various taxes. Once you retire, it's not uncommon to see that tax rate get cut in half. Typically, your overall effective tax rate goes down because your income goes down: you're controlling your income by only withdrawing what you need, and while Social Security benefits are trickling in, the amount of that check is likely going to be less than your paychecks were. So as a general rule, a person's (or a couple's) Adjusted Gross Income (AGI) decreases once they retire.

"But, Wes," you say, "my financial situation is unique. FTG won't work for me." I beg to differ. *Everyone's* situation is unique. But while your specific circumstances may be a little different than our cut-and-dry example, you can still use FTG.

I've seen people use this strategy despite variations in life: marital status, age differences between spouses, pension versus no pension, fear of stocks, fear of bonds, kids versus no kids, employee versus business owner. The list goes on. But part of the beauty of FTG is that it can be applied to anyone's retirement strategy, no matter the specific financial or life situation.

While we all have our own unique combination of variables, using the FTG strategy will help you work toward achieving your financial goals. Instead of dreading your retirement years and worrying you'll run out of money, you can rest easy at night knowing what your gap is and how you plan to fill it. If that's not a recipe for a happy, fear-free retirement, I don't know what is.

A quick note on the 1,000-Bucks-a-Month Rule: this is a very general rule of thumb to help you understand what you need to accumulate when you're young. It uses a nice round number to give you a guide for how much to save. Later on, when we talk about budgeting, we'll get a lot more specific. In Chapter 12 we'll do a deep dive on the 4 Percent *Plus* Rule, and why it matters.

DON'T LET RETIREMENT SCARE YOU

We've all heard the doom-and-gloom stories about retirement: you need millions socked away for your money to last (thanks, Suze); you'd better push your retirement age back to 70 to make sure you have enough money; if you do X without doing Y, you'll be living on public assistance before you know it.

No wonder folks these days question whether they will ever be able to retire.

The horror stories get published because they're attention grabbers—and they work because they play on our fear and insecurity about stepping into this new chapter of life. They paint reality in black and white, without allowing any room for grey.

The truth is, adjusting to retirement—especially early retirement—is not an instant process. Like anything good in life: it takes time. But that's actually not a bad thing. It simply means you are entering what I call the Retirement Grey Zone.

WHAT IS THE RETIREMENT GREY ZONE?

A lot of folks think it's either one way or the other, black or white: you're either still working, or you're retired.

That might not be so, particularly for anyone eyeing an *early* retirement. Cue the theme song from *The Twilight Zone*. You may be entering the Retirement Grey Zone.[7]

Don't worry—it's not as dramatic as it sounds. Depending on your age when you retire, you may not begin receiving Social Security immediately. Medicare enrollment may be a ways off. That pension you're so lucky to have? That may not start paying out right away either. And what about the part-time gig you've been eyeing for months?

All of these factors will play a key role in what the Retirement Grey Zone looks like for you. While each retiree's financial plan is different, there are some key fundamentals that influence income streams—those tributaries we talked about earlier—when we consider retirement-focused federal programs, pensions, and part-time jobs.

Because retirement and investment planning exist along a multiyear timeline, a day-one approach to planning often doesn't capture the entire picture. If all of our benefits and income streams kicked in the day after we retired, then, sure, planning would be a breeze.

Over the past several years, I have developed something I call the retirement timeline. This is a simple planning tool that can help anyone map out retirement, particularly those who end up in a Grey Zone.[8]

Here's the method I use with the families I help. I start by drawing a timeline: literally a straight line across the page, starting with the year you begin your planning. Then from left to right, I fill in important financial years along the way. Let's say I'm working with a husband and wife who are both currently around age 60. In our chronology, when they get to age 62 and are first eligible to receive Social Security, we may choose to add in those monthly checks.[9] At age 65, we account for the rich Medicare benefit. If either one (or both) has a pension, we mark when this benefit starts to pay out income.

Other issues make the chronology that much more important. Do you have a date set for when you want to start working part-time?[10] We can pencil that in. What about if your spouse has a different income and benefits timeline because of an age difference? We can chart that, too.

As we fill in each income stream, I also include what the couple's investment income (from their retirement savings) will be in the year they've set for retirement.[11] For ease of understanding and readability, each income stream is color-coded with a legend. With just a quick glance at the timeline, retirees can get a sense of where they are on their unique financial retirement timeline, and where they're going.

The result is a useful tool: a clear and concise one-page financial plan that maps all of the expected income resources that will kick in sometime after retirement.[12] A powerful road map for the future.

Really, just a one-page plan? Yes! I much prefer my one-page version of financial planning to an overly complicated 50-page plan. While those phone-book-size plans can be great for some retirees, they run the risk of being overly complicated and fluctuate massively with small changes to assumed rates of return and inflation assumptions. Plus, in my experience, the more complicated the plan, the more unlikely it is for families to stick to it.

In reality, most of us will live in the Retirement Grey Zone for a while. To map our way through this zone, my simple and cohesive one-page, color-coded timeline features key financial milestone dates and plots how income sources layer together. Our goal is to project the income you'll have available each month during retirement. Then you can quickly chart your budget (and fun) according to this easy-to-understand chronology.

The bottom line: fear not. The Grey Zone is a journey—"a journey into a wondrous land whose boundaries are that of imagination," as Rod Serling would say. Planning for it doesn't have to be scary. This is a time when we are easing into full retirement. We may not be traveling 24/7, but we're not working 60-hour weeks either. This translates into less pressure from work and more time to enjoy our newfound freedom.

HSAs AND THE RISING
COST OF HEALTHCARE

Unless you've been living under a rock, you know the cost of healthcare in America continues to rise. While this affects all of us, it's particularly impactful for retirees and pre-retirees.

In the 1980s and 1990s, many Americans took healthcare costs for granted. As long as you had a healthcare plan at work, the deductibles were relatively manageable because companies carried most of the weight.

Today, nearly the opposite is true, as a significant portion of large companies are switching to high-deductible healthcare plans as the rate of inflation in healthcare has skyrocketed. According to a recent Fidelity study, the average couple will need an estimated $295,000 for medical expenses over the life of their retirement—and that doesn't include long-term care.[13]

Perhaps the most practical way to plan for this is to understand the magnitude of these costs. Medicare doesn't kick in until age 65, so if you are planning to retire before that, you need a stopgap solution to cover you until you turn 65. You can get that coverage by purchasing any sort of private plan, whether through a large health insurance provider or the healthcare.gov exchange.

I strongly urge you to consider increasing contributions to your tax-advantaged accounts, especially an HSA (health savings account), if you have one. HSA contributions, earnings, and distributions used to pay for qualified medical expenses are tax-free for federal income tax purposes. If you have an HSA account available at work, contribute to it. I think of HSAs as 401(k) accounts specifically for healthcare costs.

We all know that healthcare costs are a huge part of the retirement equation. My advice is to learn more about HSAs and how they work, and then see what's available. If you're 55 or older, you can make an additional $1,000 contribution annually to your HSA.

You can take steps today to help prevent exorbitant healthcare costs from chipping away at your retirement happiness. There are solutions—you just have to know where to look.

MONEY IS A VEHICLE

Imagine, if you will, a neighborhood of happy and unhappy retirees just going about their lives. The UROB is in his lavish backyard, snacking on candy bars, admiring his BMW 7 Series while sitting beside a swampy, mosquito-infested lake. Yes, it's a metaphor. The lake represents the "reservoir" of money that—surprise, surprise—doesn't make him happy. Has he ever swum in that lake?

Absolutely not. He hasn't exercised since 1993.

On the other side of the street, the HROB is sitting in her modest backyard, admiring the brightly colored pansies she planted herself (gardening: a high-ranking core pursuit for HROBs). She's just gotten back from a brisk tennis match with her best friend (exercise and socializing: two more HROB list toppers), and is now having a gin martini with her daughter, while her grandson plays in the backyard fort (time with children/grandchildren: another HROB fave). At her feet, multiple bubbly streams of water flow like tributaries into the large river behind her house.

Yes, it's another metaphor. She understands money is a river, not a reservoir. If she gets the flow and timing just right, she can enjoy the retirement of her dreams—even if she lives to be 250 years old like an esteemed Galapagos tortoise.

At the end of the day, the purpose of having money is not just to have money. Money is a vehicle to get you where you want to go. Once you've got your Rich Ratio right and know how to Fill the Gap, you're well on your way. That means you can turn your attention to the fun part of being the Happiest Retiree on the Block: doing what you love with the people you love.

Now that the money rivers runneth, let's grab a kayak and paddle like hell to those core pursuits.

CHAPTER 4

Curiosity Habits

DEVELOP 3.6 CORE PURSUITS
(OR MORE)

A curious, adventurous spirit is the HROB's special sauce—as long as it's channeled and catalyzed the right way.

If you've read *You Can Retire Sooner Than You Think*, you probably know that for our purposes, "the right way" means "core pursuits." To illustrate why core pursuits are so important, I'd like to introduce you to Carol and Connor Calico.

The Calicos were on the cusp of early retirement when they came to see me. Carol had just turned 63; Connor, 64. Carol was a delight to work with—wonderful and warm. She was very social and had a lot of friends. She'd been a second-grade teacher for years and started drawing a decent pension when she turned 60. She decided to retire a few years later.

Carol was the perfect poster child for core pursuits. She was inherently curious. As a teacher, she had summers off, giving her time to explore everything she loved to do. But she was no slouch during the school year either. Her walking group took seven-mile hikes every Monday morning. While the rest of the world rolled begrudgingly out of bed, Carol was already halfway up a mountain. She also played tennis—and I don't mean she pulled her dusty wooden racket from 1981 out of the closet now and then. She was a member of the Atlanta Lawn Tennis Association (ALTA), the United States Tennis Association (USTA), and her local tennis club.

Now let's talk about Carol's husband. Connor was a nice enough guy, a banking and finance executive for one of the larger regional banks in the Southeast. But that high-ranking position came at a cost: in addition to being married to Carol, he was also married to his job.

The more activities Carol pursued with her friends, the deeper Connor dove into his work. In his forties he had worked insane hours; now that the Calicos' two grown daughters were off to college and out of the house, he somehow spent even *more* time at the office.

My point isn't to tarnish Connor's good name. He liked to work. Many of us do. That in itself was not the problem. The problem was the strain it put on his marriage. Carol found herself constantly nudging Connor to find more activities he enjoyed doing. I see this often: frustrated wives urging their husbands to get some damn hobbies.

Connor wanted to sit around all weekend and watch college football. That meant Carol was out in the world, feeding her curiosity and living her best life, while Connor was either at work or on the couch with a bowl of Doritos. Carol wanted to be with someone who had things to do and places to be. This led to a rift between the two that continued to widen.

After they were both retired, guess what happened? Once Connor wasn't working, the gaps in his curiosity were exposed. He didn't have any hobbies or core pursuits, and Carol didn't want to be his only lifeline. That wasn't fair to her. So after being together for nearly three decades and raising two kids—surviving years of late-night diaper changes, the terrible twos, the even-more-terrible teenage years—they got divorced.

The lesson here is simple. Carol was a happy retiree, and Connor wasn't. Their disconnect around the way they engaged with the world—with friends, family, activities, core pursuits—cost them their marriage.

Unfortunately, I've seen this story play out before. A lot of 60-year-old guys tell me, "I'm too busy for core pursuits. I can't possibly travel for fun. Once I'm retired, it'll be different." But all too often, once retirement comes, the "it'll be different" never quite bears fruit.

Core pursuits need to be developed and cultivated in advance. Plant the seeds of curiosity before you retire, so you can water them after.

Maybe you're like Carol, already nurturing your curiosity. Maybe you're like Connor, staring down the barrel of a lack of core pursuits. Maybe you're somewhere in between. Whichever camp you've pitched your tent in, core pursuits are the fuel for your campfire. My job is to help you fan the flames.

If you find yourself alarmed by the Calicos' story, don't be. I wrote this book to save you from the same tragic fate. Even though I'm an advocate for finding core pursuits early in life, it's never too late.

The good news is that core pursuits can take a hundred different shapes. Literally. In this chapter, I'll reveal the results of my research that yielded 100 core pursuits beloved by HROBs around the world.

- **The happiest retirees have 3.6 core pursuits.** The unhappiest retirees only have 1.9. We'll talk about what that means for you, and how to beef up your curiosity and sense of adventure.

- **The top four core pursuits are travel, activities with family and grandkids, playing golf or tennis, and volunteering.** Maybe you're already doing one or more of these. Terrific! If not, it's not too late to start.

- **The number one core pursuit for happy retirees is volunteering.** As luck would have it, giving to others also provides huge benefits to you. Retirees who volunteer report much higher self-rated health scores than those who don't. I've seen this in practice: HROBs who volunteer are consistently healthier than their UROB counterparts.

- **The Core Pursuit Finder can be an invaluable tool.** If you're not sure how to find core pursuits on your own, don't sweat it: there's an app for that (more on this later).

I'll also share three HROB success stories, including a married couple who couldn't be more different from the Calicos, a real-life sharpshooter—and a man I call Safari Sam.

But first: what exactly *are* core pursuits?

CORE PURSUITS: YOUR HOBBIES ON STEROIDS

Core pursuits are the building blocks for happiness during your post-career years. They're like hobbies, but *bigger*. In other words: they're your hobbies on steroids.[1]

As a quick refresher, the difference between a hobby and a core pursuit can be explained this way: A hobby is reading an article from *American Fencing Magazine* every once in a while and taking a one-day fencing class at a nearby university. A core pursuit is joining a local fencing team and starting a weekly podcast called

En Garde that charts the career of Hall of Fame Olympic fencing coach Maitre Michel Alaux in his quest to approach the sport as both an art and a science.[2]

Our survey findings show that *HROBs have 3.6 core pursuits*, whereas UROBs have 1.9 (Figure 4.1). So if you already love to play golf, make cheese, and fence, you can become 0.6 of a cowboy poet and you've hit your 3.6 quota. Mission accomplished!

Of course, it can take a little more effort in real life. Some people believe working was the hard part, and all they have to do for a happy retirement is kick back and not lift a finger. This, my friends, is simply not the case. You have to know what you want to do during your retirement years before you can enjoy doing it. Sleeping in and sitting on the porch are nice perks, but a happy and fulfilling retirement they do not make.

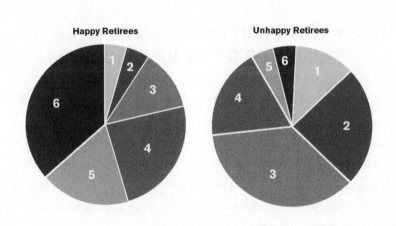

FIGURE 4.1 **Number of Core Pursuits of Happy vs. Unhappy Retirees**

That's why you need core pursuits. These are the activities you're really passionate about, the ones that bring you excitement and a sense of fulfillment while you're doing them. Core pursuits are what make HROBs feel most alive.

And they're not just for current retirees, by the way. They're for people in their thirties, forties, and fifties as well. I'll say this all day long: I believe it's critical to find your core pursuits *before* retirement.[3] The sooner you develop them, the better. In addition to upping your happiness quotient once you reach your golden years, they'll help you save and invest better because you have a purpose for your money.

No matter how far you are from retirement, now is the time to start exploring your curiosity, developing your core pursuits, and engaging in them wholeheartedly.

Which brings us to our next question: What types of core pursuits are right for you?

FROM PICKLEBALL TO BONSAI: ALL KINDS OF CORE PURSUITS

To answer that question, I knew I needed to delve deeper into what people choose as their core pursuits. If you know me at all, you know how much I like surveys. So I did a mini-experiment. I sent a survey to all 50 of the folks at my company, asking them to tell me some of the most memorable core pursuits they'd come across while working with our clients. It was a fun exercise, and we came up with quite a list.

Most of the core pursuits fell into four categories. There was *part-time work*, like teaching, consulting, and decorating. Then there was *exercise and health*—activities that included hiking, biking, swimming, walking, and cooking. The *arts* were a big one, with painting, pottery, and music topping the list. And then there was *adventure*, such as travel, cruising, RVing, piloting, and sailing.

Take a look and see if any of the core pursuits from the Top 100 List (Figure 4.2) catch your eye, either because you're already pursuing them or would like to.

There may be 100 core pursuits on this list, but the options are endless for the happy retiree. The only limitations are your creativity and openness to trying new things. Sure, you can be a real go-getter and attempt all hundred, but you don't have to. The only requirement is three or four at a minimum. Just don't do zero!

Skydiving	Walking	Squash/Racquetball	Stained Glass
Piloting	Running	Citizen Patrol/Fire Fighting	Competitive Dancing with Dog
Archery	Travel (Cruise, National Parks)	Sculpting	Movie Making
Car Racing	Cooking	Antiquing	Animal Adoption
Yoga	Volunteering	Learning New Instruments	Custom Razors
Tennis	Concerts	Learning New Language	Button Making
Golf	Art (Drawing, Painting, etc.)	Teaching/Coaching	Animal Training
Wine Tasting	Bowling	Photography	Mahjong
Hiking	Swimming	Farming	Leatherwork
Knitting	Blacksmithing	Water Polo	Fencing
Quilting	Cowboy Poetry	Fox Hunting	Horseback Riding
Gardening	Civil War Medicine	Acting	Home Brewing
Sewing	Scrapbooking	Tour Guiding	Triathlons
Fishing	Book Writing	Car Collecting	Courier
Camping	Pickleball	Pottery	Chick-fil-A Cow Mascot
Church (Choir, Bible Study)	Birdwatching	School Bus Driver	Historic Ship Model Building
College Football Games	Gambling	Shooting Range	QVC/At-Home Shopping
Spending Time with Grandkids	Model Trains	Geology	Bonsai Tree Care
Crossword Puzzles	River Cruises	Start a Band	Paper-Mache
Reading	Sailing	WWII Club	Social Clubs
Book Club	Marathons	Dinner Murder Mystery Clubs	Making Cheese
Attending Theatre Productions	Camper Road Trips	War Reenactments	Collecting Samurai Swords
Skiing	Interior Decorating	Pinochle	Online Gaming
Bridge	Water Aerobics	Classic Car Restoration	Palm Reading
Bingo	Shuffleboard	Missionary Work	Enneagram
Biking	Needlepointing	Woodworking/Whittling	Podcasting
			Grilling

FIGURE 4.2 **Top 100 Core Pursuits**

I VOLUNTEER AS TRIBUTE

Did you know that adults over the age of 55 make up 25 percent of the volunteer workforce annually? I suspect most of those people are either HROBs or well on their way.

Volunteering provides rich social, mental, and physical benefits. The Beatles once sang, "the love you take is equal to the love you make." I'm not sure if Paul McCartney was thinking about retirement when he wrote that line—he was, after all, only 27—but considering his extensive philanthropy and charity work in his later years, I think it's safe to assume Sir Paul knows giving back is a great way to get back to where you once belonged.

Opportunities to Make an Impact

If you're looking to get involved in your community, consider these 10 ways to lend a helping hand:[4]

1. **Tap your professional skills.** You've spent the last 20, 30, 40 years honing your expertise in a certain field or industry. Why not take those same skills and put them to use in a not-for-profit way?

2. **Use your trade skills.** Are you a carpenter? An electrician? A landscaper? Offer your time or services at a charity auction or community fundraiser, or simply pitch in when a friend or neighbor needs help.

3. **Let your creative energy flow.** If you're a musician, start a volunteer band that plays for USO tours. If you're an artist, share your artwork at the local hospital. If you're a

performer, put on a new play. Lend your voice and your talent to causes you care about.

4. **Become a member of a board.** Board members have a powerful opportunity to impact an organization by becoming deeply invested in what happens behind the scenes.

5. **Help people with their taxes.** Ben Franklin said it best: nothing is certain except death and taxes. You can't always help people with the first, so why not try the second?

6. **Get your hands dirty.** Clean up a highway. Plant some trees. Beautify your neighborhood in places the city won't. Better yet, build a house for a family that needs it. Or take a cue from my Amish friends and raise a barn.

7. **Tutor someone.** Are you good at algebra? English? Photoshop? Maybe there's a kid nearby who could use your help. Or maybe it's a peer who can't figure out their new MacBook Pro!

8. **Help a senior.** Ask the senior citizens in your life how you can best assist them. That might mean weed-whacking their hedges or shopping for groceries if they're homebound.

9. **Spend time with animals.** If you can foster a rescue dog or cat, fantastic. If you can't, offer your time and energy instead. Who wouldn't want to while away the hours in a puppy pile of love?

10. **Do your own thing.** Maybe it's social entrepreneurship. Maybe it's something no one has thought of yet. If you see a volunteer need that's not being met, fill it.

> Any of these options could spark your interest in a new cause you never knew existed. As you get involved in whatever way feels right and sustainable to you, it will inevitably generate greater joy and fulfillment in your life.

Volunteering is win-win, because it's good for other people *and* good for you. Think of all those who've adopted a rescue animal. Once Sparky is trotting around the house, begging for walks and bones, rare is the HROB who says, "I saved Sparky." More often, they say, "Sparky saved *me*."

Don't take my word for it. A 2019 independent report by the Corporation for National and Community Service (CNCS), a federal agency responsible for the nation's volunteer and service efforts, stated that: "Senior Corps volunteers report much higher self-rated health scores, which is considered a valid marker of actual health, compared to older adults in similar circumstances who do not volunteer. They also reported feeling significantly less depressed and isolated compared to non-volunteers." Senior Corps is a United States government agency with the mission of providing aid to senior citizens in communities while promoting a sense of community.

Check out these amazing statistics from AmeriCorps:[5]

- After two years of service in the Senior Corps, 84 percent of older adults reported improved or stable health.

- 32 percent of Senior Corps volunteers who reported good health at the beginning of the study reported improved health at the two-year follow-up.

- Of those who reported five or more symptoms of depression at the beginning of the study, 78 percent said they felt less depressed two years later.

- 88 percent of Senior Corps volunteers who first described a lack of companionship reported a decrease in feelings of isolation after two years.

- Among those who initially reported a lack of companionship, 71 percent reported an improvement in their companionship status.

Volunteering is good for your health. Full stop. I encourage every retiree and pre-retiree I work with to volunteer for a cause they believe in.

Now let's meet some real-life HROBs and see how different retirees interpret, find, and engage in core pursuits.

NED AND NANCY NATIONAL: THE HAPPIEST RETIREES IN THE PARK

Ned and Nancy National are from Birmingham, Alabama. When they retired five years ago, they had no visions of green golf courses and pickleball tournaments. Instead, they wanted to take on the National Park Challenge and see *all* of America's 63 national parks.[6] Now we're talking!

The National Park Challenge is not for the faint of heart. Take, for example, Virgin Islands National Park. In addition to being off the beaten path, it is regularly hit by devastating hurricanes. Or consider Wrangell-St. Elias National Park, which sits in an isolated corner of southeast Alaska and is bigger than Yellowstone, Yosemite, and Switzerland *combined*. Even more extreme: Gates of the Arctic National Park has no roads and requires taking a chartered flight above the roaming caribou.

What do all of these parks have in common? Three words: *Ned and Nancy.*

Ned and Nancy are determined to visit all 61 national parks—even Kobuk National Park, which is located entirely above the Arctic Circle. Picture a dune-filled desert like the Sahara, only with wolves. The Nationals have now tried to access Kobuk twice; both times, summertime snow and sleet turned them away. But they were undeterred. Why? Because they are HROBs, and HROBs are insatiably curious. They crave that feeling of accomplishment, and after two failed attempts, they only want to visit Kobuk *more*.

––––––

Tackling a challenge like this takes an adventurous spirit and a heavy dose of planning. Ned and Nancy have hit about 12 parks annually for the past five years. It's certainly not logistically easy or cheap. But the experience has been magical, and, as they confess, it's made the past half-decade of retirement particularly worthwhile.

"But, Wes," you say, "that's only *one* core pursuit. Didn't you say the happiest retirees have 3.6?"

To which I reply: you're exactly right. But here's the bonus perk of something like the National Park Challenge: it actually comprises multiple core pursuits nested under the main one, Russian doll style. America's national parks are found from coast to coast, across nearly 30 states and two US territories. Every stop invites visitors to bike, climb, swim, drive, play, eat, hike, camp, and explore. Ned and Nancy aren't just passively viewing the country through the windows of their RV (though camper road trips certainly make a great core pursuit). They are engaging in multiple core pursuits on every new adventure.

It's easy to imagine the social interactions and cultural variety they experience on these trips. Ned and Nancy have no shortage of good conversation as they reflect on the people they meet and places they see. What better way to avoid a daily rut of fast food and daytime television?

Fun fact: I've also found that the happiest retirees take 2.4 vacations annually versus 1.4 for their unhappy peers. Nearly double! The happiest folks prioritized vigorous exercise, travel, and family time, too.

A National Park Challenge–like adventure sets you up for all of this: travel, adventure, and breaking a sweat.

Let's say that, after reading this book, you decide Ned and Nancy National are your new personal heroes. You feel so inspired by their story, you choose to chart a similar course. Maybe you're not aiming for all 61 national parks, but you are going to hit the road and have a grand adventure. Good for you!

While it doesn't necessarily have to break the bank, there are definitely big line-item expenses to plan for.[7] Ned and Nancy bought a middle-of-the-road RV and have put over 125,000 miles on it. While RVs range from around $100,000 to seven figures, a solid one can be financed and become a dependable mode of transportation for years to come.

Maybe, after a year or two driving around America, you'll decide that being a road warrior isn't for you. That's fine, too. Trade it in, and you're probably only out of pocket for the cost of one big vacation.

Beyond the RV itself, expenses like park admissions, parking, and campground fees can add up. Don't sweat these or let them deter you, but do account for them. You could look for ways to swap expenses. Trade or pause your gym membership and get your workouts in as you hoof it through nature. Pause your cable and opt for a cord-cutting option like Amazon Prime or Netflix if you need some on-the-road entertainment.

Also, check out great senior discounts that reduce park fees.[8] At the time of this writing, the America the Beautiful senior pass only costs $80 for a lifetime, unlocking admission to more than 2,000 federal recreation sites in addition to all national parks.[9] In most cases, a pass covers entrance, standard amenity fees, and day-use fees. At many sites, it affords the pass-owner a discount on expanded amenity fees (such as camping, swimming, boat launching, and guided tours). Sounds like a lot of core pursuits all rolled into one!

So what'll it be? Zion, Shenandoah, or Mount Rainier? Sixty-three of the world's most beautiful destinations are waiting for you, not to mention the 2,000 other appealing recreational attractions. Start an adventure, stay moving, get social, and accept a challenge like this for a lifetime of memories. Let Ned and Nancy lead the way.

VINNY CARR:
TINKER TAILOR SOLDIER GUY

Maybe you're not into nature or national parks or driving an RV around the country. That's fine. I'm not kidding when I say there's no way to choose the wrong core pursuits. You just need to have at least 3.6 of them.

Take my friend Vincent "Vinny" Carr. Vinny wasn't keen on gallivanting around the country. His interests were a little closer to home. The only problem was: he didn't have enough of them. By his early sixties, he really only had one or two activities he enjoyed doing outside of work. When he came to see me about a year before he retired, he knew he needed to make some changes, stat.

So Vinny picked up target shooting. He hadn't shot much previously, but he found it was something he really enjoyed doing.

These handgun competitions—sport and target shooting—were great, but still not quite enough for him. So Vinny dug deeper. He discovered an entire circuit of sport shooting in the South. He attended more and more of these competitions and started moving up the ranks. He went from 110th place to 60th to eventually finishing in the top 10.

Vinny's diligence and fervor for target shooting paid off in other ways, too. At the competitions he met people from all over the Southeast. Vinny is a very likeable guy, but before he got into shooting, he didn't have a very large social network beyond his neighbors and the people he worked with. Suddenly, thanks to his new core pursuit, his social network expanded, enriching his life.

He didn't stop with the gun competitions. He also decided to rebuild his 1965 Chevy Camaro. He allowed his curiosity free range by asking the question, "Can I pull this off?" Not only was he rewarded by a feeling of accomplishment once it was finished, he gained even more happiness by taking that car to shows, events, and clubs. Vinny met even more people as he went the extra mile with his core pursuit. Make that extra *miles*.

Are you beginning to see how multilayered core pursuits can be? One can lead to the next, which leads to the next, which leads to the next, and suddenly, you're a 3.6-core-pursuit happy retiree, bragging to your unhappy neighbor about all the cool things you're doing with your life.

If you're *still* thinking, "This is all great in theory, Wes, but I just don't know how to put core pursuits into practice. I don't like hiking, I hate guns, and Camaros make me sick."

Don't worry—there's an app for that.

Actually, it's a quiz.

FIND YOUR CORE PURSUITS:
IT'S AS EASY AS A, B, C

A common question I hear from readers and radio callers is, "How do I find the core pursuits that light me up inside?" People are ready to set sail, but they don't know where to turn their rudders. Which is exactly why I designed the Core Pursuit Finder.[10]

Drawing once again from the rich well of my happy retiree base, my team and I complied an extensive list of HROB core pursuits. As you might imagine, there was plenty of overlap with the Top 100 List. Then, using their personal preferences, I created an algorithm.

Who among us doesn't love a good *Buzzfeed* quiz? I, for one, am not immune to its charm. So, building off the algorithm, I created a *Buzzfeed*-style quiz designed to plumb the inherent curiosity, capacity, and interests of every aspiring HROB.

The process is painless. You answer a few simple questions, zeroing in on your personal preferences, and the algorithm populates a customized list of core pursuits. The questions aren't complicated. For instance, would you prefer your core pursuits to be outside or indoor activities? Answering that one question can tell us a lot.

The next thing the Core Pursuit Finder asks is if you'd like to give back to society. If so, with time or money? Or maybe not at all? The quiz doesn't pass judgment. It simply holds up a mirror to your likes, dislikes, natural inclinations, and curiosity. Each selection winnows down the list until you're left with core pursuits that fit like a glove. Who knows? Maybe you'll even discover a new passion for glove making.

The Core Pursuit Finder is uncannily accurate. And I'm not just saying that because I developed it. Recently a 36-year-old colleague took the quiz, assuming it wouldn't be able to read her personal preferences since she's a long way off from retirement—and it read her like a book. She said it was actually unnerving how spot-on the list of core pursuits was. Some she was already pursuing: teaching, coaching, writing. Others were exactly the ones she'd been wanting to start: selling crafts on Etsy, interior decorating, amateur taxidermy.

"Wes," she told me, "I will never doubt you or your algorithms again."

Are you starting to get the picture? The Core Pursuit Finder is a simple and powerful way to kick-start your own curiosity. You can even start a side hustle and have it count as a core pursuit, as long as you can do it on your own terms. When part-time work becomes a core pursuit, you get the bonus of another revenue stream in retirement that simultaneously gives you a greater sense of purpose and pleasure.

You can always try another core pursuit if one doesn't work out. You may love golf, but some pesky lower-back pain demands you take a break. No need to fret. Time to replace golf with yoga so you can heal the muscle tightness. Maybe it's temporary—or maybe you'll love yoga so much that you'll keep the bird of paradise along with the birdie forever.

Core pursuits are like happy retiree insurance. So whether it's racquetball, squash, pickleball, tennis, book club, bingo, bridge, pottery, or driving a school bus, give it a try. That's what HROBs do.

SAFARI SAM: MAN, LEGEND, HROB

There's no better way to end this chapter than with Safari Sam.

Sam is one of my all-star clients, the textbook definition of the Happiest Retiree on the Block. He recently took a three-week trip to Kenya and Tanzania with his wife and nine friends. It was such a life-changing experience, he felt compelled to email me afterward:

> We all found ourselves retired at the same time and with "traveling funds" from our retirement accounts. We scheduled the African safari trip together—and it turned out to be one of the most memorable times of our lives. We were

all animal lovers with a fondness for the rare rhinoceros, so we named our 11-member traveling group the "Chubby Unicorns" in honor of the rhinoceros and had T-shirts made accordingly.

Safari Sam and his wife have always loved traveling, so it was at the top of their core pursuits list in retirement. The only truly difficult part of their journey was trying to pick a favorite picture to send! Sam said it was like trying to pick a favorite child.

After much deliberation, they came up with an amazing tableau of trampling tuskers (Figure 4.3).

FIGURE 4.3 **Safari Sam's Elephant Herd**

Sam's wife took this photo at dusk. The elephant herd was returning home across the plains in front of Mount Kilimanjaro in Tanzania. You can see Kilimanjaro in the background, shyly peeking out from behind some cloud cover and providing a striking background for these lovely, gentle giants. As spectacular as this was, it was just one of many memorable sights they saw on this incredible trip.

Sam and his fellow Chubby Unicorns took another photo in front of their beloved rhinos. When he was looking back at the pic, he realized that 6 of the 11 in the group were working with advisors at my firm.

As Sam put it, the Chubby Unicorns were a "living, breathing advertisement" for us. Call it a shameless plug if you want, but I can't tell you how much that means to me. We love what we do, and a big part of what we do is helping retirees become HROBs. Of course I love the positive advertising, but even more than that, I love that the core pursuit concept is taking hold and changing lives. Safari Sam and his Chubby Unicorns have committed to being HROBs—and they've got the pictures to prove it (Figure 4.4).

FIGURE 4.4 **The Chubby Unicorns**

Curiosity is the key to happiness in retirement. It's the key to not getting a divorce in retirement. It's the key to . . . everything in retirement. Those 3.6 core pursuits (or more!) can add years to your life. For those of you who worry you are biologically incurious, I'll offer some easy advice and a firm little nudge. *Core pursuits don't just happen—they must be cultivated, strengthened, and expanded over time.* Again, just like saving money, positive gains don't come overnight. But the sooner you start, the happier you'll be.

So get an RV and strike out on an adventure. Play golf. Volunteer at a women's shelter. Restore a classic car. Go to Africa. Or choose one of the lesser known core pursuits from the Top 100 List. Brew something. Start a murder mystery club. Don an animal costume and be the mascot for a local team. Better yet, create your own combination of activities that allow you to nurture your curiosity, be active, expand your social networks, and stay young.

It doesn't matter what you do. As Nike famously said, "Just Do It."

CHAPTER 5

Family Habits

GET YOUR KIDS OFF
THE PAYROLL

"**Family is not** an important thing. It's everything." So said actor, producer, and legend Michael J. Fox. Considering he went back to the future, then back again, I believe him.

Most retirees, whether happy or unhappy, have children and grandchildren. It stands to reason that "good" and "bad" family habits reveal themselves in *how* retirees interact with their kids and grandkids, namely how independent or dependent those kids and grandkids are.

The habit at the heart of this chapter is deceptively simple: *HROBs don't need to support their adult children financially, and their adult children are not still living at home.* There are some troubling statistics that we'll tackle, like a CNN report showing 52 percent of young adults in the United States are living with their parents.[1] Or the staggering findings from my own money-and-happiness data: *over 40 percent of families* are giving their adult children some level of financial support.[2] This doesn't include children with special needs, of course, or the occasional gift of plane tickets or birthday cash. I'm talking about support from parents to subsidize their everyday lives—private schools, car leases, rent, mortgages, college loans, paying down debt, and so on—because the kids don't make enough for their lifestyles.

Personally, I believe this is the biggest retirement problem no one talks about: when kids are still on the payroll. It happens when retirees are still bankrolling the financial immaturity of kids in their twenties, thirties, or forties—and it happens far more often than you'd think.

Here's a brief snapshot of the findings from my recent research:

- **On average, happy retirees have 2.5 kids.** Unhappy retirees have 0.5 kids. Having half a kid may sound straight out of the Old Testament, but I promise there's a way to interpret this data in a positive way.

- **Keep your kids off the payroll.** At the very least, give them a pay cut. They need to be financially independent of you, and vice versa.

- **Kids should get married and get out.** Retirees are twice as likely to be unhappy if their adult children are not married. Retirees are also twice as likely to be unhappy if their adult children still live at home.

- **Live near at least 50 percent of your kids.** Your kids shouldn't live *with* you—but at least half of them should live *near* you. Retirees who live "near or close" to at least half of their children are five times more likely to be happy.

- **Overeducating your kids is overrated.** We want our kids to be educated, but at a certain point, it starts to take a toll on happiness. There's an interesting trail-off in retirement happiness once the adult children begin to pile on multiple degrees.

In this chapter, we'll dig into each of these habits in more depth. If I could boil them down to one essential piece of wisdom, it would be this: when it comes to family, the key is finding the balance between connection and freedom. If you've ever found yourself enjoying a pleasant Thanksgiving dinner until that one cousin cornered you to talk about how the moon landing was fake, you understand how important balance can be. As humans, we need and crave connection, but it's important not to get overserved.

Spoiler alert: the big lesson of this chapter isn't much of a secret. The goal is to raise a close-knit but independent family. Having children is an important part of this. On average, happy retirees have 2.5 kids. Unhappy retirees have 0.5.

Am I suggesting that you birth half a kid? No. I'm just saying that somewhere between two and three is the elusive happiness target. My research indicates that having fewer than two tends to correlate with higher levels of unhappiness.

If you're reading this book, I'm going to go out on a limb and say you may already have the number of kids you're going to have—or have decided to have none at all—and there's not much to do about it. As luck would have it, I'm right there with you. To illustrate that these happiness habits aren't an exact science, I'm going to tell you a personal story.

IT'S NOT (JUST) ABOUT THE NUMBERS (OR HOW MY WIFE KNOWS BEST)

After we had our son Jake, our third child, we were smack in the middle of the baby phase but finally seeing a light at the end of the tunnel. He'd started to sleep through the night more often, and I no longer needed quite as many shots of espresso to get through the afternoon slump.

One day, I was sitting at the kitchen table, working on my last book, when my wife, Lynne, came in and said, apropos of nothing: "If we're going to have a fourth kid, we better do it soon. We're not getting any younger."

"Speak for yourself," I said. "I shot a 40 on the back nine just last week." Translation: I'm in my prime, baby!

She wasn't buying it. I had to pull out the big guns.

"I'm literally working on a chapter about how happiness levels are heavily influenced by the number of children retirees have. Look at this!" I pointed to the screen. "My research shows diminishing margins of happiness after the third child."

She glared at me, unimpressed, like I was a third grader working on a book report.

"It's like you're a third grader working on a book report," she said.

"But the data is clear!" I exclaimed, fully aware I was proselytizing. "We've got three kids. We're golden."

If you think I won the argument, I assume you've never been married. I may be a retirement Sherpa to my clients and readers, but in my own house, I'm just my wife's assistant.

And thank God that's true because we now have a beautiful fourth child named Samuel.

As my own story shows, there's no perfect number to adhere to for any of these habits. No HROB keeps exclusively HROB habits. We're all human. We're not going to check every box perfectly, nor should we try. The goal is simply to adopt as many traits of the happy retirees as we can. Just because we might have one habit that aligns with the unhappy retiree doesn't mean it ruins the stew. The number of kids is only one ingredient. Luckily, it's not the most important one.

At the core of family habits among the happiest retirees is one linchpin issue: supporting your adult kids.

STOP FINANCIALLY SUPPORTING YOUR CHILDREN

Right now in America, the cost of living can be alarmingly high and career income opportunities seemingly low. Case in point: at the height of the Covid-19 pandemic in mid-2020, the unemployment rate skyrocketed to 14 percent, the highest it's been since the Great Depression. And despite our economy's tremendous recovery, many families today are faced with the dilemma of adult children who need more financial support than they may have in the past, a common refrain among the people who call in to my radio show.

"Hey, Wes, my son is 35 and he's doing OK, but needs some help."

"My daughter is 42, and she can't afford to send her daughter to private school."

As parents, we all want to help. But how much help is healthy for them *and* for us?

Here is where the aforementioned CNN article by Catherine E. Shoichet in September 2020 comes into play.[3] Shoichet sourced a Pew Research Center study that found a whopping *52 percent* of young adults in the United States are living with their parents (Figure 5.1).[4] It's the highest percentage since the Great Depression. No wonder parents are depressed.

Pew defines "young adults" as 18- to 29-year-olds, and says that the number of those young adults living with their parents grew to 26.6 million in July 2020. This number is staggering to me.

All parents want the best for their children. But there must be limits and boundaries for reasons both emotional and financial. As stated earlier, my recent money and happiness study of nearly 2,000 retirees nationally found that *over 40 percent* are giving

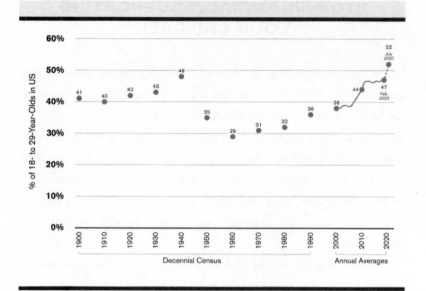

FIGURE 5.1 Adults Aged 18–29 Living with a Parent
Note: "Living with a parent" refers to those who are residing with at least one parent in the household. 1900–1990 shares based on household population.
Source: Pew Research Center analysis of decennial census 1900–1990; Current Population Survey annual averages 2000–2019; 2020 Current Population Survey monthly files (IPUMS).

their adult children some level of financial support. This type of "help" walks that fine line between assistance and enabling.

Check out the striking data from Pew Research about the number of parents who support their adult children financially in some capacity shown in Figure 5.2.[5]

These findings suggest nearly 6 out of 10 parents are offering some type of financial support to their children over the age of 18. The poll also showed that at least some of the financial help was geared toward recurring expenses. The money was going toward household expenses such as groceries or bills, and a significant share used it to help pay tuition, rent, or mortgage. While the

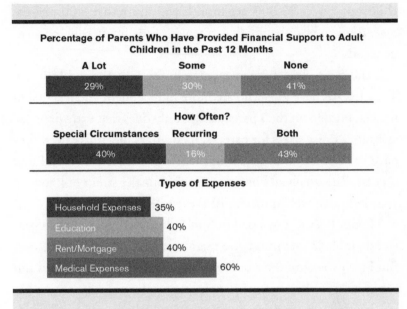

FIGURE 5.2 **Six-in-Ten Parents Financially Supported Their Adult Children in the Last Year**
Note: "Adults aged 18–29" includes only those who reported having at least one living parent. "Parents" includes those aged 30 or older who have at least one adult child aged 18–29.
Source: Survey of US adults conducted June 25–July 8, 2019. Pew Research Center, "Majority of Americans Say Parents Are Doing Too Much for Their Young Adult Children."

educational requirement for knowledge worker employment today makes it difficult to expect full financial independence for an 18-year-old, the trend is a concern.

While parental instincts are difficult to keep in check, the impact of this support may have a devastating effect on finances *and* levels of happiness. My research suggests that the unhappiest retirees overwhelmingly responded that they still support adult children, averaging over $700 per month, while happy retirees kept that figure to under $500. At the extremes, a couple supporting adult children at over $2,000 per month was more than 400 percent *more likely* to be unhappy than one with fully financially independent kids.

There is a clear difference between the HROBs and UROBs. The HROBs have kids who are more independent and less of a financial burden on their parents. Not only does that extra financial assistance cause stress for parents, it counters the innate need they have to see their kids go out in the world on their own and find success. The financial burden is tough, but the strain of knowing your kids aren't self-sufficient runs even deeper.

Look, I get it. I'm a dad of four kids under 21. I want to protect them, help them, and give them every opportunity to succeed. But I have to count the cost of this support. It's not just dollars and cents; it's my wife's and my happiness at stake.

It's a matter of setting up rules and guidelines, with the knowledge that they aren't set in stone. Some rules you'll need to stick to; others can change as your circumstances evolve.

When I think of a family that has done an excellent job of making rules that are both strong and flexible, the Dineros come to mind.

MEET THE DINEROS: PARENTS OF THE YEAR

Don and Dorothy have three very bright kids. It's something they've always prided themselves on as parents, raising their two sons and one daughter to be curious—and to boldly explore that curiosity wherever it might lead. The Dineros made a commitment to each of their children: they would pay for their college tuition. But after that, if their kids chose to continue their education through grad school, law school, business school, or what have you, it was up to them to fund that dream.

All three kids went to good colleges, where they thrived. The eldest son, Diego, had always been a dreamer. He majored in American literature at Emory. The Dineros' younger son, Domenic, had a knack for winning every argument; he studied law at Georgetown. And their daughter, Diana, had spent her whole life tending to sick pets and patching up her brothers' skinned knees, so it surprised no one when she announced she was premed at the University of Georgia.

When Diego graduated from Emory, he worked for Teach for America. Then, in his mid-twenties, he went through a brief period of unemployment during which he moved back home. He toyed with the idea of going to grad school to study comparative literature or philosophy, but even with a grad student stipend, he would probably need to keep living at home.

Don and Dorothy made their position very clear. Their son could live with them for six months, and after that, he would need to make other arrangements. Diego accepted those terms. Within two months, he had decided against a lofty PhD and secured a job as a copywriter at a local ad agency. It was a good job, with nice benefits and an even nicer paycheck. After saving up for three months, Diego moved into his own apartment—a whole month ahead of schedule.

Since Domenic and Diana were studying law and medicine, they would need to continue their studies postgrad to practice as a lawyer and pediatrician, respectively. Dom took a gap year and traveled before coming back to Georgetown for law school, while Diana went straight through, staying on at UGA.

Dom and Diana both needed a little help with tuition. They weren't asking their parents to absorb the entire cost, just to subsidize it. After a lot of heart-to-hearts—and several meetings with me to look over their finances and reexamine their earlier rule—Don and Dorothy decided to do everything they could to get their kids over the education finish line and off the payroll. They helped, but they set a limit.

Before you shake your finger at me, remember: these rules aren't immutable. They don't have to be ironclad. Circumstances change and life throws curveballs. Don and Dorothy wanted their two youngest kids to flourish in their respective fields, and that meant readjusting the framework they had erected 20 years prior, when it was all just theory. But they did it wisely, with an eye to their own health and security, and enlisted my help.

Today, all three of Don and Dorothy's kids are in their mid-thirties, independent and out of the house. Diego is an adjunct professor at a liberal arts college and does freelance copywriting on the side. He's happily married with three kids. Domenic is a successful lawyer at a nationally recognized firm, and he just proposed to his girlfriend of two years. Diana loves her work as a pediatrician and is a great mom to her three-year-old daughter. All three of Don and Dorothy's kids live in the state of Georgia, so they're pretty close but not on top of each other.

The Dineros have maintained a family lake house for three decades, and the whole family goes up together several times a year. Don and Dorothy love spending that extra time with their grandkids. Then, when the fun is over, they go back to their respective homes. This is the epitome of close-knit, but independent.

YOU SAY "I DO"; THEY SAY "I DON'T"

Today people are getting married later in life or not at all. A new study from the Institute for Family Studies showed that the US marriage rate hit an all-time low in 2019. For every 1,000 unmarried adults in 2019, only 33 got married. This number was 35 in 2010 and 86 in 1970.

These statistics play into the concept of independence. At first blush, it might seem like getting married later means people are *more* independent, pursuing their careers, traveling, and having varied experiences out in the real world.

I hate to burst your bubble, but that's just not the case.

The fact that people are marrying later or not at all is, I believe, part of the reason the Pew study showed 52 percent of young Americans still living at home. If we wait to get married, then it's more likely we delay striking out on our own.

I like to use driving as an example. Think about how you felt when you were a teenager. I bet you couldn't wait to get your driver's license and own your first car so you could go more places and be more independent. Today, that sense of urgency is lacking. Who needs a car if you can just call an Uber?

Being a grownup is not necessarily about age. It's about your level of responsibility. When you're married and you have a child, a mortgage, and a job—and you start seeing big taxes come out of your paycheck—you get a crash course in maturity. And, according to a Gallup poll taken a few years ago, it's a course fewer and fewer Americans are choosing to take (Figure 5.3). That may be why later generations don't have quite the push that the previous generations have had to get up and get out.

For a parent, your level of confidence goes up when you know your kids are OK. When they're still living at home, that can cause some apprehension about their future. I'm not suggesting that having adult children at home will *always* lead to unhappiness; I'm just interpreting the data. And the data is clear: retirees are more likely to be unhappy if their kids are not married and/or living at home. The kids of HROBs tend to get married, and move out—not necessarily in that order.

Here's the raw deal: You can't force your kids down the aisle. Can't make them fall in love. Can't even make them start dating.

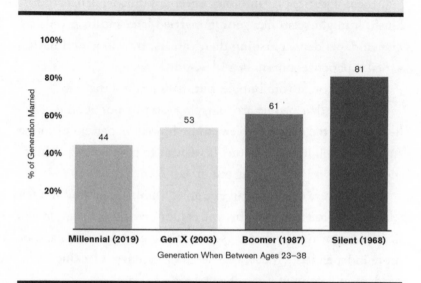

FIGURE 5.3 **Percentage of Generations Married Between Ages 23–38**

Note: A person is considered to be in a family if they reside with a spouse, their own child (including those who are biological, adopted, and/or stepchildren), or both. Adults with a spouse who is currently living apart from them (but from whom they are not legally separated) are considered to be living with that spouse from this analysis.
Source: Pew Research Center analysis of 1968, 1987, 2003, and 2019 Current Population Survey Annual Social and Economic Supplement (IPUMS). Pew Research Center, "As Millennials Near 40, They're Approaching Family Life Differently Than Previous Generations."

You can give little nudges every now and then, dropping some wisdom about the virtues of marriage and the beauty of finding a life partner. It's natural to want that for our kids. And of course, the subtext of those desires is that we also want them to be emotionally and financially independent, so that we don't carry the full burden of providing for them once it's time for us to redirect our resources toward our own lives.

My point is this: Your children will do as your children will do. And it may not include "I do." Who knows? Maybe one of my sons will choose not to get married. Maybe, God forbid, all four will. And if that happens, will I cry over the boutonniere I will never get to wear? No. I will do my damnedest to practice the other habits that will contribute to me and my wife being HROBs to offset my four defiant sons auditioning for *The Bachelor*.

Now, are you ready for the catch-22? Because as much as we want our kids to be up, out, and independent, we also want them to be close enough for visits. That's right, you read that correctly. We want our adult children to get married, live their lives, and go away . . . but not *too* far away. And if they do, watch out, because we'll be right behind them.

YOU CAN'T GO HOME AGAIN—BUT YOU CAN MAKE A NEW HOME

This is my favorite one of the family habits. Maybe because, unlike playing matchmaker for your kids, it's something that *is* within your power. While you can't control whether or not your kids get married and how soon, you *can* control how close you live to them.

Proximity to your adult children is pivotal for HROBs: it's important that you live near your kids (Figure 5.4). Think driving distance. Put another way, if Jim and Cara have four kids and live in Atlanta, they are more likely to be happy if three of them live in the state of Georgia, even if one of the children now lives in Los Angeles.

I'd been working with Frank and Ava Johnson since they first came to see me in their forties. They were college sweethearts— Frank went to Morehouse College, Ava to Spelman—and after they met at a school mixer one Saturday night, they never looked

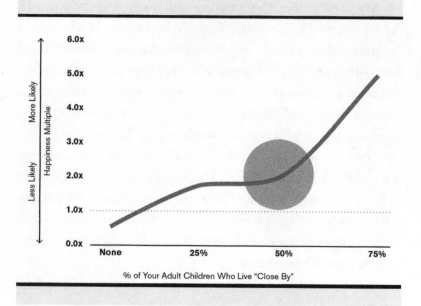

FIGURE 5.4 **Live Near the Kids**

back. The Johnsons spent their whole lives in Georgia, very happily so, and retired a few years early. Their daughter moved to Florida for work, and their son moved to Washington state. Frank and Ava realized that they wanted to be near their daughter in Florida, so they bought a house in the same neighborhood and really loved it down there.

The Johnson family had a good couple of years in the Sunshine State, eating oranges and spending time with their grandbabies. Then their daughter was transferred to California, meaning both of their adult kids were on the West Coast.

Frank and Ava were still young retirees, in their mid-sixties. They had lots of energy and plans for the future. They decided to go back to Georgia to do all the things they'd always wanted to do. They told me, "This is going to be our time!"

Case closed? Not so much. Six months in, they realized that despite all the freedom and lack of babysitting commitments, something was missing. They yearned for the days of being really close to their kids and grandkids. But they felt guilty about it.

"Wes," they said, "we shouldn't have to be close to our kids to have a happy retirement. We don't want to impose on them."

But the Johnsons weren't imposing on their kids. Both their son and daughter were excited about the idea of their parents moving to the West Coast. I see this often: adult kids don't view it as a burden when their parents move closer. It's actually the opposite. Not only do they enjoy seeing their parents more—and the free babysitting—it's a relief to them that their aging parents will be easier to reach if they need help and support.

So I told the Johnsons to give themselves permission. I was adamant.

"Ava! Frank! You want to move to California to be in the same general area as your kids? Heck, yes! Do it!"

This need to be stoic and deny yourself the happiness of being near your kids? That's not what happy retirees do. I told them to trust their instincts and the instincts of their kids. Make it happen!

Six months later, Frank and Ava told me moving to California was the best decision they'd ever made.

HROBs have the flexibility to do what they want to do. They have the financial resources to make big decisions, including big moves. By giving themselves greater freedom and security, they make room for greater joy.

PUT YOUR HANDS UP AND STEP AWAY FROM THE PHD

The final area I want to cover is what the data shows about the amount of education for your kids. *Overeducating your kids is overrated.* I found this really interesting and unexpected. Of course, we all want our kids to be educated, but at a certain point, it takes a toll on our happiness. Why? Well, let's examine that.

At first glance, retirement happiness and even longevity seems to rise with education levels. Essentially more education is better for a variety of reasons.

In fact, in an interesting article I found from Wharton titled "The Increasing Mortality Gap by Education," you can clearly see that those with education levels beyond high school consistently had a lower mortality rate than those with just a high school degree (Figure 5.5).

You might then be wondering how higher levels of education could actually be a bad thing. Don't we all want to live longer? Yes, but it turns out the old axiom about "too much of a good thing" applies even to education.

If your kids didn't graduate from high school or stopped directly after being handed that diploma, you are likely to be an unhappy retiree. Families with college-educated-and-beyond children saw the highest happiness levels. But here's the breaking news: happiness levels begin to decline in families in which the adult children received doctorate degrees.

Remember our friend Diego Dinero? The dreamer who was contemplating going back to school to philosophize about Kant and Nietzsche? Imagine if he'd gone after that PhD in philosophy, signing on for an extra 6 to 10 years wandering the ivory halls of academia. And what if, horror of horrors, he had expected Don and Dorothy to foot the bill?

It's hard to live your best life on a fixed or reduced income when the tuition jackals won't stop nipping at your nest egg. It's different if an advanced degree results in an appreciable skill set or professional qualifications, such as Domenic's law degree or Diana's MD. But when you're writing monthly checks because

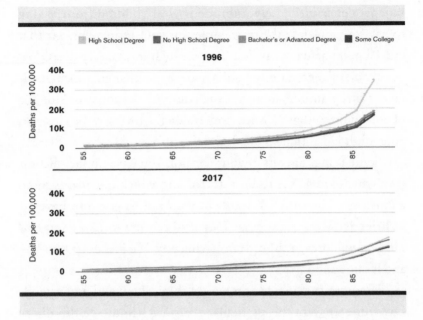

FIGURE 5.5 **Mortality Rates by Year and Age by Education Levels**
Source: Osorio Victoria, "The Increasing Mortality Gap by Education"
(blog post), Penn Wharton Budget Model, Penn Wharton, University
of Pennsylvania, July 6, 2020, https://budgetmodel.wharton.upenn
.edu/issues/2020/7/6/mortality-gap-by-education

Junior wants to be the foremost authority on Friedrich Nietzsche,
it's easy for resentment to rear its ugly head in your subconscious.
If Junior wants to spend his life contemplating nihilism, more
power to him. But he's got to pay for that himself.

I believe happiness levels typically rise with education because
more education often opens more doors to independence for your
kids. It gives them options once they leave the nest, which is great.
But if instead of leaving, they bring the books and bills back to the
nest, the branch will break. It's not sustainable for you, and it's not
good for them.

In case you're ever feeling selfish about setting a firm line on how
much assistance you give your adult children—don't. Your own

independence ultimately unburdens your children from having to pay for you when the time comes for your retirement. Let that crucial point assuage any guilt for painful but necessary decisions.

None of these family habits are easy to change overnight. It takes time, planning, finances, and courage. Getting your kids out of your house? That's a huge undertaking. Moving to be closer to your adult kids? That's a big deal.

Some things are out of your control. You have no jurisdiction over which kid wants to be a doctor and which one wants to be a musician. You can't tell if one of your kids is going to have 10 girlfriends by the time he's 21 or if his shrine to *Dungeons and Dragons* will prevent him from having any. We just don't know— and it's not up to us.

However, there are factors we can think about and understand. Over time we want this particular statistical habit to go this direction versus that direction. Let's say two of your three kids live in Charleston, South Carolina, but you still live in Allentown, Pennsylvania. Your focus should be, over the next five years, how do you get to Charleston? Structure is your friend.

We'll end this chapter where we began: with Michael J. Fox. The guy's not wrong: family really is everything. But if *Back to the Future* isn't your thing, maybe take a cue from *Fast & Furious*. No matter how many mistakes Vin Diesel makes or how many death-defying risks he takes, he never forgets how much he loves his family. If Vin can keep his family close, I can say with confidence he'll be a happy retiree by the time the fortieth sequel rolls around.

CHAPTER 6

Love Habits

GET MARRIED—OR *RE*MARRIED—ONLY ONCE

I've been in the investment planning business for more than 20 years. When I work with couples over that long a time period, it's not all sunshine and kittens. There are bumps in the road. So it's not that uncommon for a couple to ask (usually separately and covertly), "Hey, Wes, can I afford to get a divorce?"

I first remind them I am not a marriage counselor. If they need proof, my wife is always happy to provide a few embarrassing anecdotes. (For the record, I still contend that a North Carolina Tar Heels jersey is a romantic anniversary gift!)

Despite being a perpetual student in my own holy matrimony, I do have an answer to the question, "Can I get a divorce and still be a happy retiree?" And it might surprise you.

In this chapter, we'll look at my fascinating findings on marriage and divorce, and discuss how these reflect the lifestyle and financial habits of the happiest retirees. We'll also talk about being single, and whether or not that damns you to the unhappy side of the street.

You'll learn that:

- **If retirees are not married, they are 4.5 times more likely to be unhappy.** That's a pretty big variant, proving there's a significant link between marriage and happiness.

- **When it comes to marriage, one do-over is just fine.** Turns out you *can* get divorced without negatively impacting your retirement happiness—but only once. Everybody gets one marriage mulligan if you need it.

- **Happy retirees discuss—but don't obsess over—money.** Money is often cited as one of the top reasons people get divorced. The trick is to strike a healthy balance between keeping the financial conversation open, but not so open that it swallows you whole.

- **The marriage timeline can be a great guide to the peaks and valleys of marital bliss.** This can be comforting when you're at a less-than-happy part of the curve. Like the stock market, if you just stick it out a little longer, you'll catch the next updraft.

- **Happy retirees make time for sex.** It's no secret that no sex is a quick path to frustration. And although HROBs don't necessarily report sex like newlyweds, having sex at least once a month is a good baseline; otherwise levels of unhappiness begin to rise. If activity rises to several times a week, you're twice as likely to be an HROB. So get busy!

- **You can still be a happy retiree if you're single.** It's statistically harder, but it can be done. If you're a party of one, it is essential that you are very intentional about your support networks and staying active, connected, and socially engaged with your family of choice.

Let's get the biggest, baddest statistic out of the way first. *If retirees are not married, or have never been married, they are 4.5 times more likely to be unhappy.* Your marital status does have a major impact on your likelihood of being an HROB. And while you don't need to be married to be an HROB, you do have to work harder to be happy if you're single.

Of course, as is true with all the habits in this book, they're meant to serve as general guidelines, not a prescription. There are often other, more complex variables at play that deserve a seat at the table.

If you're single, either by choice or by circumstance, feel free to flip ahead a few pages to get to the good stuff. If you're married, like the majority of my readers and radio listeners, then stick around. We're going to take a deep dive into the ocean of marital bliss.

"But, Wes," you say, "if you're telling me I have to be married to be happy . . . what if I'm *unhappily married*? Does that mean I can't get a divorce?"

To which I say: you're in luck.

YOU ONLY GET ONE:
THE TRUTH ABOUT DIVORCE

Remember how I said my answer might surprise you? Well here it is: *divorce is actually OK—as long as you only get divorced once.*

Marriage takes practice, and you don't always get it right on the first go. Our research shows that there are high levels of happiness associated with being married one time—*and* two times.

In other words, you can take one mulligan. After that, you're headed for UROB-ville. Happiness levels begin to fall once you've been married three times or more. But rest assured that having a divorce on your résumé doesn't necessarily lead to unhappiness in retirement.

I realize that this advice goes against the grain of what other books might tell you. Typically, when we imagine "millionaires next door," they've been married to the same person forever. *The Millionaire Next Door* is actually one of my favorite money books of all time, and in it, the late Dr. Thomas Stanley discusses the importance of being married—and *staying* married. But Stanley is much more focused on sheer wealth accumulation habits than the balance between wealth and happiness.

Jay Zagorsky, a research scientist at Ohio State University's Center for Human Resource Research, writes, "Divorce causes a decrease in wealth that is larger than just splitting a couple's assets in half."[1] Zagorsky's study of about 9,000 people found that divorce reduces a person's wealth by about 77 percent. On the other hand, it showed that being married almost doubled comparative wealth (93 percent).

My findings don't deny the obvious cost, financial and emotional, of getting divorced. But they do challenge the assumption that those costs always equate unhappiness. Divorced folks *can* be happy retirees. Rather than telling you never to get divorced because of the financial devastation, I'm telling you there is more than one factor to consider. Yes, you want to avoid losing money—but you also need to consider happiness.

I don't want you to be just rich. I want you to be rich *and* happy. Because if you aren't happy, then what's the point?

I'll admit that, in spite of all the research I did for my last book, I never fully contemplated what effect divorce had on happy retirees. Yes, it can be financially devastating, and there are a lot of other problems that come along with it, like higher expenses, long-term alimony, custody battles, child support, and hefty attorney fees. If you have kids and are sharing custody with your ex, it means you're less free to move to a different city or take a job opportunity in another state. There are obvious and multiple downsides to divorce. I get that. But is one divorce devastating to retirement happiness? My research shows a resounding no.[2]

Again, I'm not a marriage counselor. Before you start running profit margins on a theoretical divorce, maybe you should start by talking to your spouse. One of the things you should talk about is money.

Guess what? There's a right way and a wrong way to do that, too.

MONEY: THE ELEPHANT IN THE ROOM YOU SHOULD ACTUALLY TALK ABOUT

Almost 70 percent of Americans say they'd rather talk about their weight than their money.[3] It's right there on the Thanksgiving-dinner taboo list with politics, sex, and opinions about in-laws. Obviously, my in-laws are all wonderful, which is important to say, in case any of them are reading this.

As anyone who's married knows, there are things you have to talk about, things you want to talk about, and things you have to talk about precisely because you don't want to talk about them. For many couples, money falls into this third category.

Is it any wonder the *Huffington Post* found the topic of money is among the top five stresses on a marriage?[4] We all have different views on money, forged by our culture, our families, and the way we grew up. When our views are different enough from our spouse's, it can cause a disconnect.

That's exactly why you *must* talk about it. If money stays in the realm of the room elephant—never mentioned, never discussed—you're setting your marriage up for unhappiness.

The happiest married retirees *discuss—but don't obsess over—money*. There's a fine line between paying attention to and obsessing about your financial situation. As is often the case, balance is the secret sauce.[5]

Retirees who reported never discussing their finances (zero hours per month) are twice as likely to end up in the unhappy camp, whereas happy retirees spend between one and two hours a month talking about their finances: retirement savings, mortgage balances, car payments, paying off debt, location for retirement, healthcare costs, and so on.

Beyond 2 hours a month—and up to 3.5 hours a month—happiness levels plateau. After 3.5 hours a month, "money talk" can actually be counterproductive, as we see happiness levels decline. It's clearly healthy to discuss money, but talking too much about your finances or harping on your budget excessively is a bad sign.

In other words, address the elephant in the room, but do not lavish endless attention on it.

MARRIAGE AND HAPPINESS: A ROLLER COASTER

We've made it to my favorite part of any chapter: the data. I love conducting research because it's an attempt to explain the complicated world we live in.

In my most recent national research study, I asked retirees to tell me how many years they'd been married to their current spouse. The results ranged widely: anywhere from 1 to 40+ years. There were also questions designed to gauge happiness levels, and the results showed some strong and fascinating trends.[6]

Informed by my data, I've created a marriage and happiness timeline (Figure 6.1) to help show some familiar progressions, the

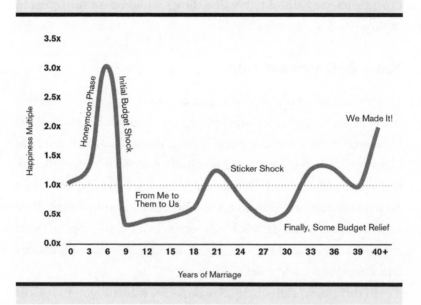

FIGURE 6.1 **A Happiness in Marriage Timeline**

good and bad times of a union between two people. The timeline reflects the money challenges, hard realities, and financial ups and downs common to each phase of life.

My theory is that this marriage and happiness timeline applies mostly to a long, single marriage. Our research is still TBD on these cycles in marriage number two or beyond. But regardless if you are in marriage one, two, or three, the following is an eye-opening guide to how money might impact your particular stage of marital bliss.

While this isn't a habit, per se, it can yield considerable insight into the natural fluctuations of marital happiness. If you're feeling unhappy in your marriage, it can be a comfort to know you're not alone and that there are proven trends, an organic ebb and flow of contentment. If you currently find yourself in one of the downturns, it's helpful to see that things could be on the upswing in time.

Years 0–6: Honeymoon

Double income, no kids, low expenses. Need I say more? The first phase of marriage can be blissful. Ah, yes, I remember those days. How were things more affordable back then? Well, that tends to happen with two incomes and no children to feed. These folks are colloquially known as DINKs: double income, no kids. They have no parental responsibilities and low financial commitments. They aren't paying for diapers, schools, or summer camp. Spending is mostly in check, and the marriage is new, so everything is chocolate, champagne, and roses.

In this phase, cash outlay is reasonable, student loan payments (which vary with income levels) remain low, budgeting is straightforward, and, in many cases, that burdensome mortgage is still a ways out.

It's no surprise then that folks in this stage reported that *happiness levels were robust*. Their responses suggest a profound sense of newness, fun, and freedom. They enjoy the novelty of having a special someone to adventure with. Even though it's an adjustment, this period is perhaps the easiest financial stage of marriage.

Most parents can't even remember how much freedom they had during this phase. Perhaps they've mentally blocked it, which might be a necessary survival tactic during the later years of sleep deprivation and screaming babies.

Years 7–9: Initial Budget Shock

The bloom is off the rose. Time to buckle up, happy couple.

Once you've got kids, all of life's major expenses start to hit hard. Not only do childcare and the cost of school add up; it's possible you're paying for it with only one income. Or if not, then some sort of daycare is involved. If multiple children are in the picture, expenses quickly start to multiply. You're growing your family, which is great. But financially, you're going through multiple shocks.

I've had so many of these conversations with younger people who are trying to plan. It's a hard transition. After the initial honeymoon phase, happiness generally takes a big hit. It would be weird if it didn't!

But as I said, I don't want to get into the marriage counseling side of this. I want to help you prepare for the financial implications that accompany each period. For couples in this stage, happiness is in free fall because there are new surprises around every corner. The cash previously spent on adventures and romantic experiences is swallowed up by no-fun necessities. Would you rather visit the Louvre in Paris or search three drugstores in one night to find the only kind of baby butt cream that doesn't give your kid an allergic reaction?

Adding to the stress of these expenses is that most couples aren't exactly swimming in savings just yet. Pushing your budget to the brink each month when you're only buying necessities is bound to make you a little cranky. And as if that weren't bad enough, because your income is just starting to rise a little, student loan payments come a-knockin'. Also, when you move out of your hip two-bedroom townhome in the city to the fixer-upper house with a yard, you don't just get a leaky roof: you get a sizable mortgage. Oh, and if—*when*—something breaks, guess who the landlord is?

When my wife and I had our first son, I remember viewing everything through a sticker-shock haze. Does the price tag on that jogging stroller really say $400? School lunches cost how much? They were only $1.50 when *I* was in school! Maybe we'll skip soccer camp this year . . . except that will mean a lot of tears since all our son's friends are going. How can such tiny people need so many doctors? And why is the deductible on our family health insurance so high?

Expenses pop up from every angle, all larger than expected. You and your spouse are getting hit from all sides—and unfortunately, that's not a sexual innuendo. Sex got put on the back burner about 800 diaper changes ago.

Hang in there. The good news is that this phase only lasts about two years. After that, a new one begins.

Years 10–22: Calm Seas

The storm has finally subsided, and to your own amazement, you managed not to capsize your vessel. Once you get into year 10 of marriage, happiness begins its long, slow, choppy voyage toward the beautiful sunset on the horizon.

You're now able to spend more time and money on you and your spouse. What a relief! Your happiness levels start to rise a little. You've hit a stride. Buying strollers is a distant memory. You might be able to afford a private school tuition bill. If not, that's fine. About 88 percent of kids go to public school and are doing just fine.

In this stage, the spending goes from flowing directly into the diaper mill to a sense of, "Hey, let's take a trip together!" You all want to see the national parks, or maybe you take a Disney cruise together. It's not just about what the kids want. It's what you all want as a happy family unit.

For what it's worth, happy retirees reflect on this time as an emotionally satisfying period. I know this because I've asked them. Income was starting to go up, the vacations were getting a little better, and the family experiences were more memorable now that the kids were showing their unique personalities, already growing into their adult selves.

From my own personal experience, I can tell you that the older your kids get, the more they interact and the more fun everybody is. As they mature, they become more than tiny creatures you need to keep alive. They become people you actually enjoy.

In this stage, you're starting to let your kids become a little bit more independent. They love it, of course. So do you, but you play down the fact that letting them drive means you don't have to chauffeur them around town. Their self-sufficiency ticks up incrementally, and with it, so does your reserve of free time, energy, and disposable income. Once they hit high school, they might even have their own jobs and no longer require an allowance to buy every single item. Is this heaven?

It might as well be. After years of feeling like platonic business partners in charge of Offspring, LLC, you and your wife are actually attracted to each other again. Bring on the mood lighting and scented candles, 'cuz we are *back*.

Years 23–27: Midlife Crisis

All of a sudden, there's a dip in happiness in this 23–27 year phase. My theory is that your kids are starting to leave the house, and empty nest syndrome hits hard. Your kids moving out is a huge adjustment, a whirling black hole of love and companionship.

You've probably had kids for about 18 years at this point. Then they go off to college. Of course, you miss them, but the emotions are only one aspect. Having worked with many retirees over the years, I can tell you it's a really big financial hurdle to get over.

Let's say you've got two or three kids in college around the same time. You go from free public school to tens of thousands of dollars per year per child. This is all the scarier because around this time you're starting to eye retirement. You know their education is worth it, but there's no way to sugarcoat the financial damage—it's often bigger than the mortgage.

So here you are with a double whammy: the emotional stress of kids leaving the nest and the massive hit to your retirement plan and cash flow. It makes for a rough patch financially, and it can impact marital happiness.

It's important to mention that at this stage, your quasi-adult children want to be independent, and you want them to be. But how much can they really afford? Full-time college students don't have full-time jobs. This can often lead to having them on the payroll, like we talked about in Chapter 5. You might end up with a tug-of-war about "How much should they pay versus how much should we pay?" The right answers can be murky.

You're not alone. It's a tough call, particularly in that 18–25 age range. When they're 18, sure, you want to help them eat those meals. But by 25, aren't they supposed to be out and about?

The trick here is to set boundaries, sticking to them and adjusting as needed. You're up against a cultural phenomenon of kids "growing up" later, but as we saw in the last chapter, there are ways to buck the trend.

Years 28–39: In Too Deep

Now we're starting to see some budget relief. Hallelujah! Here's some great news: happiness starts to rise for the rest of our lives. At this stage, couples really begin to see the light at the end of the tunnel, financially and otherwise. The kids are now self-sufficient or getting more so. They're off the payroll. Staggering college tuition payments stop. You start to have some money for yourselves again. You get some disposable income back and can really start accelerating retirement savings.

While relief continues, your career might be in fifth gear, going well. Typically, this is when you've got more autonomy and freedom, and you're making more money. You're developing more and more core pursuits as you start to have the time, with one eye toward retirement. Maybe your passion or side job has more room to blossom.

Years 40+: We Made It!

Happiness goes through the roof in this stage. We see from our research that happiness returns to honeymoon phase levels. Couples have finally settled in or hit their stride. They are more acclimated now than ever to the cost of life in America.

Couples experience a sense of gratitude, anticipation, and joy. At this point, these folks are retirees in their sixties and seventies, enjoying their little grandkids. I've found that the vast majority of retirees take great pleasure in being grandparents because it's a lot less difficult than being a parent. The phrase I hear a lot is, "You can see 'em and then send 'em home." Very true. I can't wait to be a grandparent.

At this point, couples have typically identified what their retirement plan and income will look like. Their budget starts to relax because the mortgages are paid off or close to it. Sometimes couples find more affordable housing—not necessarily downsizing but perhaps moving to a different area that's less expensive. A cycle of freedom and autonomy abounds with progressively fewer financial constraints.

Folks end up having the time and the financial bandwidth to invest in the people and projects they really care about. Volunteerism goes up, and those experiences provide a sense of purpose and wholeness.

I hope it's obvious by now that not every marriage follows this timeline, especially the ones that are not ultimately successful. As Leo Tolstoy famously wrote, "Happy families are all alike; every unhappy family is unhappy in its own way." We all know people who were married a long time and either grew apart or were never a fit and only stayed together for the kids. Maybe they went through a divorce that was hard and painful for a year, but ultimately it was the right decision. Afterward, their happiness eventually went up.

When you're getting married for the second time, usually later in life, you don't have to go through the difficult initial budget-shock phase that so many new marriages go through in years 7 to 9. If you get hitched when you're on the 15-year+ marital upslope, you get to skip some steps.

Let's Get It On

In my most recent retirement study, I asked about sex. I wasn't sure people would answer . . . but they did (Figure 6.2). No, I'm also not a sex therapist, and the topic has never come up in retirement planning with the families I work with. But in an effort to dive deep into the fascinating world of romantic relationships and retirement happiness, I thought it would be irresponsible not to at least ask.

The results probably won't surprise you. If you're not having sex, it's not great. You're almost two times more likely to be unhappy.

Remember, the baseline is to have sex at least once a month to land in the happy camp.

And if you can clock in at least once a week? You're smart *and* sexy, because you're twice as likely to be happy.

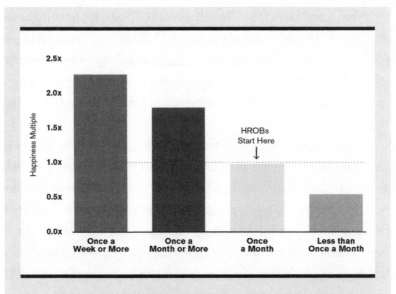

FIGURE 6.2 **Sex Frequency and Marital Happiness**

I know from personal experience that it can be hard to make the time. But it's always been worth it—at least for me. When my youngest son, Samuel, was just three months old, my doctor pulled me aside and said, "Wes, I know it feels like life is all about the kids right now—and you've got four of them! But do not in any way forget about the bond you have with Lynne. Just because you're one shy of a basketball team, you can't be too busy to have intimate time with your wife."

What can I say? I did what the doctor ordered.

IT'S OK TO BE SINGLE—AS LONG AS YOU'RE SUPPORTED

As we've seen: if you want to be an HROB, the statistics show it does help to be married.

That said, if you find yourself without a mate, it's not all gloom and doom. If you're single by choice, it doesn't necessarily mean you're resigned to unhappiness—you can still successfully retire *and* be happy. And if you're single *not* by choice, it might just be a matter of biding your time until you meet the elusive Mr. or Mrs. Right.

The delightful Katie Carter, who first came to me in her mid-forties so we could start planning her retirement, became a widow at 56 after her husband died two years into his retirement. She stayed single for a while, confident that if she were to find another partner, she would know exactly who and what she'd want. Katie was looking for someone within driving distance who had a similar lifestyle (not someone who would take advantage of her wealth) and who was highly active like her. We're talking about a woman who's hiked the Himalayas and the Andes. She had no interest in the liars on dating sites who said they hiked or played golf, meaning they played once 10 years ago.

After getting clear on what she was looking for (and not looking for), Katie gave online dating a chance. She was able to narrow it down to 10 interesting guys. From there, she winnowed the list even further to three legitimate candidates, with whom she went on three legitimate dates. At that point, she understood pretty quickly that there was only one lucky fellow who checked all the boxes for real.

After a year and a half of dating, Katie Carter is now married and in a long, upward honeymoon phase.

Some people wait years after losing a beloved spouse to remarry. Some might never remarry. And others have chosen to never get married at all. There's nothing inherently wrong with being single. But if you do choose to stay single, it is essential that you have a supportive network. Whether it's friends, family, or ideally both, these connections will keep you firmly on the HROB side of retirement.

The single people I know who are happy retirees have one thing in common: *they are very intentional about their support networks*. In Chapter 8 we'll talk about how Dan Buettner, while researching his book *Blue Zones*, discovered that it's part of the Okinawan Japanese culture to have a Moai: a group of five friends for life. These people are your family beyond your family, your "family of choice" instead of your "family of origin." Who knows? Maybe you'll be even happier. Most of us don't get to choose our families! Even when we wish we could.

The happy singles I've been lucky to know and work with all follow this same path. They're very active and very deliberate about staying connected and engaged socially with friends. I think if you're really intentional about that, it does offset the statistics that claim you need to have a partner.

So whether you put a ring on it long ago, have traded up for a second set of rings, or are choosing to fly solo, know that the financial and marital bumps in the road eventually lead to a wonderful place.

Just one final word of advice: Ditch the Tar Heels jersey as an anniversary gift for your wife. She went to University of Kentucky!

CHAPTER 7

Faith Habits

BELIEVE, GIVE, AND DO GOOD

I wish I went to church more. I really do.

If you read the Preface, you know I grew up in a small town outside of Lancaster County, Pennsylvania. Technically, I was raised as a Quaker. Also known as Friends, Quakers are a denomination of Protestant Christianity, and though there are various movements within the larger faith, they share a fundamental belief in every human being's God-given ability to access the light within themselves.

In other words, Quakers are the original hippies.

I still remember how much this fascinated my college friends back in Chapel Hill, North Carolina. "Wes," they'd say, after a couple of cold ones. "What's it like when you go back home? Do y'all even drive? I thought Quakers could only drive those horse-and-buggy things."

That was when I realized that Southerners thought I was Amish.

I wasn't offended. My family wasn't particularly devout. What I remember most from my upbringing is that Quakers don't believe in fighting. Peace is huge for them. Beyond that, I don't have a lot of vivid memories. We went to church twice a year at best.

If you've never been to a Quaker church service, you don't know what you're missing. You basically sit in complete silence, sometimes for hours on end, until someone is moved to speak. Now that I have four kids, that kind of silence sounds like a slice of Heaven. Of course, when I *was* a little kid—back when all I wanted was to be at home watching cartoons like my non-Quaker friends—it felt more like Hell.

Flash forward to adulthood. My wife hails from a Lutheran family in Michigan. After Lynne and I got married, we joined a Lutheran church in Atlanta, but we didn't really know anyone. Then we moved to another part of town and enrolled our kids in a Presbyterian preschool. We became active in supporting the school, which led to joining the church, and in turn we met dozens upon dozens of wonderful families. Great pastor, great community, and all in all, a successful "conversion" from our humble Quaker-Lutheran beginnings to our new Presbyterian home.

I would go to church every single week if I could. I honestly get so much from it. Unfortunately, having four small children and a Sunday radio show keep me a little too busy to win the perfect attendance award. Let's hope God doesn't keep track of those things.

This is a book about retiring happily, not a book in which I evangelize. I'm certainly not trying to push any specific religious affiliation on you—much of what I'll be sharing in this chapter is anecdotal, a product of my own spiritual journey. As your favorite research guy, let me reassure you that there's no data on which religion produces the happiest retirees. But I *will* say there seems to be a connection between having faith, giving back, and being happy.

In this chapter, we'll discuss how:

- **The happiest retirees attend church on average once a week.** They're 1.5 times more likely to be happy than other retirees. Go less than once a week and your likelihood of landing in the happy camp begins to taper off. This is one of those habits on which I'm dropping the ball myself. Lucky for me, my God is a forgiving God.

- **Going to a place of worship can be a powerful way of building community.** Losing access to social networks is one of the greatest risks during retirement. Even if you're on the fence about what you believe, getting involved in your local church, synagogue, mosque, or temple will give you access to a larger community of good people doing good works.

- **HROBs both believe and give.** While you certainly don't have to attend church to start volunteering, the two often go hand in hand: most faith-based communities have ample opportunities for retirees seeking to dedicate their time, energy, resources, or all three to worthy causes.

If you're not a believer, keep reading, because this chapter also talks about volunteering on its own merits. I will say, though, that in my humble opinion, the Lord is good. If you're asking yourself, "How in the hell can I be happy in retirement?" I say, try a little heaven.[1]

IT ISN'T *WHAT* YOU BELIEVE—IT'S *HOW*

First, some bad news. Church attendance has declined in recent years. According to a study from Pew Research Center, only 45 percent of Americans who attend religious services say they attend monthly or more. In 2009, that number was 52 percent.

(Figure 7.1).[2] In fact, the same study says that 17 percent of Americans say they never attend religious services, up from 11 percent a decade ago.

You could blame a number of factors for the decline: busy lives, the entanglement of faith and politics, an increasingly secularized society. I'm not qualified to weigh in on why or how we got here; that's not my bailiwick. But what I *can* say with confidence is that, once again, happy retirees are bucking the trend.

As part of my expanded research study, I asked thousands of retirees how often they attended services at their place of worship. Once I crunched the numbers, I made the lovely graph in Figure 7.2.

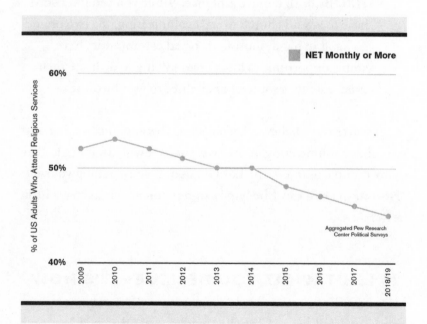

FIGURE 7.1 In the United States, Church Attendance Is Declining
Source: Pew Research Center Religious Landscape Studies (2007 and 2014). Aggregated Pew Research Center political surveys conducted 2009–July 2019 on the telephone. Pew Research Center, "In U.S., Decline of Christianity Continues at Rapid Pace."

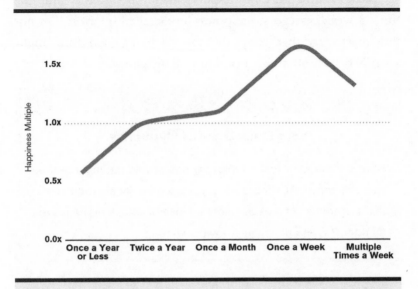

FIGURE 7.2 **Happiness and Religious Attendance**

If you are a person of faith who worships regularly, bless you: *the happiest retirees attend a religious service an average of once a week*. In fact, weekly service attendance makes you 1.5 times more likely to be happy than non-attendees.

There is also a bare minimum when it comes to annual attendance. Happy retirees go to church at *least* twice a year. Come Christmas and Easter, you know where to be! Even a guy like me with four kids and a radio show goes to church more than twice a year. Again, I'm not setting any attendance records, but I go as much as I can. I love our church; it keeps me accountable and interested. When I've attended other churches in the past, I haven't always felt that way. Sometimes, the key is to find a great church so that attendance doesn't feel like a mandatory box you have to check, but rather something you look forward to every week.

Back to the data. Once respondents jumped to the "multiple times a week" category, happiness levels tailed off a bit. I'm not sure how to read this, except that too much of a good thing might actually be . . . too much. Just don't tell my pastor.

Your Daily Dose of Hypocrisy

Here's some juicy insider info: my pastor told me most people who *say* they go to church every week actually average something closer to 1.7 times per month. A pastor who deals in uneven numbers? That's a man after my own heart.

Going to church plays a larger role in some parts of the country than others. I happen to live in the South, which is technically referred to as "the Bible Belt." But I've never felt like anyone is beating me over the head with religion. You don't have to be part of a church to fit into Southern culture, though it does grease the wheels a bit.

In my 40-year pilgrimage from Quaker to Lutheran to Presbyterian, I look in the rearview mirror and ask myself, what good qualities do they all have in common? Turns out the answer is pretty simple: there is power in faith. For thousands of years, people have found great comfort in believing in something greater than themselves. I think we can all find that in our own way.

Which brings me to my next point: the power of community.

LOVE ONE ANOTHER, AS I HAVE LOVED YOU

If you read *You Can Retire Sooner Than You Think*, you may remember how much I love my friend Dan Buettner's book *Blue*

Zones: Lessons for Living Longer from the People Who've Lived the Longest.[3] Buettner introduces us to a community of 9,000 Seventh-day Adventists in Loma Linda, California, a group of people who live almost a decade longer than the average. The way they do it is through a myriad of life choices, but for Buettner, one of the pivotal factors behind their longevity is that they create and maintain a loving and connected community.

I am obviously not saying you have to be a Seventh-day Adventist to be happy in retirement. What I *am* saying is that it's increasingly rare for me to meet an HROB who doesn't have any sort of involvement with a faith-based community.

Ready to hear something that may be controversial? I hope it isn't blasphemous—though if I'm struck by lightning before the next paragraph, you'll know why.

Maybe it doesn't matter so much *what* we believe, but *how* we believe it—and *who* believes it alongside us. I think the particular belief system isn't anywhere near as important as the aspect of community it offers its believers.

There is a tremendous capacity within any community. We get to know our neighbors, friends, and other families who are all a part of a community that extends beyond our work or home life. Being able to come together with like-minded individuals gives us ample opportunities to make significant connections and meaningful relationships. And what better community than a place of worship? A church or synagogue becomes a kind of "social epicenter," one of the keystones of social connectedness. (We'll talk more about getting and staying connected in Chapter 8.)

More than just a general connection, a faith-based community allows for several generations to learn from each other. The young 'uns learn from the oldies, and vice versa. This kind of socialization is a little less myopic than your average social, athletic, or hobby group. Being part of a community of believers can allow for multigenerational bonds to form in a way that's impossible in social settings where you're surrounded by peers who are similar in age.

Personally, I've found there to be something extra meaningful about meeting my friends' parents, as well as their kids. At our church, I see many grandparents connecting with people of all ages. I don't have the specific stats on how this plays out in retirement—that'll be part of my next research project—but anyone with eyes can see that these sorts of connections are conducive to health and happiness. They create constant opportunities to nurture a sense of purpose and find the unique ways you can touch the lives of others.

Then there is the most glaringly obvious way being part of a faith-based community syncs up to happiness in retirement: volunteering. *HROBs both believe and give*. Volunteering gives retirees the feeling of meaningful accomplishment that is hard to replicate outside of acts of service. It's no surprise the happiest retirees love donating their time and energy to great causes—and there's no easier place to volunteer than through your place of worship.

I'm not saying you have to be a regular service attendee to volunteer. But my work has shown there is a definitive link between volunteering and faith. Places of worship can provide multiple in-roads for service opportunities that you may not have thought of on your own. There's a whole vibrant world behind the scenes of every religious service that has far less to do with dogma and far more to do with walking dogs for homebound elderly community members, or building houses for people who need them, or whatever form of service speaks to you.

A typical place of worship in America will offer opportunities to get involved with a number of causes and underserved groups. These might include working with underprivileged children, food-insecure communities, and people suffering from homelessness or mental illness. You could seek out opportunities to work with women's shelters or animal rescues. Or if you prefer to pitch in at your place of worship directly, volunteer for religious education, prayer groups, or camping trips for parents and kids.

Every church I've ever been a part of—and this goes back to the Quaker meeting house where we would sit in silence for hours watching the clock tick—incorporated volunteer projects into their weekly offerings. An active place of worship will provide various opportunities to help the larger community. My church here in Atlanta feeds food-insecure folks up to five times per week. They also administer a program to help women who are in abusive relationships. There are toy drives, presents for foster kids at Christmas, a social entrepreneurship program, and much, much more.

In sum, I don't know of anything that makes it easier to find opportunities for service than a thriving faith-based community.

INVESTING IN THE CAUSES
YOU HOLD DEAR

I want to touch on one of the most common ways of giving, which is to invest monetarily in the causes you hold dear. It can be easy to get caught up in our busy lives and neglect to donate to worthy causes. This is one thing I like about going to church: the weekly reminders to tithe. But you certainly don't need to be passed the collection basket to give.

I've found it even easier to put my giving through some sort of charitable donor-advised fund (DAF). A donor-advised fund is a way to put money away today in the current tax year, obtain a current-year tax deduction, and then allow the money to grow on a tax-deferred or tax-free basis over time. The technology of the donor-advised fund has gotten so good that you can utilize it as a platform to direct that money to one or more charitable institutions, including your place of worship. A DAF is a good way to put your giving on autopilot, which is powerful whether you want to funnel your money to a church or any other charitable organization. In my opinion, Fidelity[4] and Schwab[5] both have great DAF options.

We all clearly get some sort of physiological benefit from giving, and this is a great way to do it. When we give, we feel we are actively participating in society. Even more than that: we are leaving it better than we found it.

That's a significant part of the HROB story. Retirement is not meant to be you living in your castle high on a hill, hoarding the fruits of your labor. Ebenezer Scrooge was most definitely not an HROB. A happy retirement provides multiple opportunities to give back, whether from the riches in your savings or the new-found riches of your time. The ultimate irony is that giving away some of those riches enriches you as well.

THE "HEY, HONEY" TEST

Before we move on to social habits, I'd like to close this chapter by introducing what I call the "Hey, Honey" test. This is one of my favorite litmus tests, an invaluable tool in any married or partnered person's toolkit.

If you want to casually test the waters of a new course of action in theory before putting it into practice, I highly advise you to lean on the wisdom and foresight of your beloved spouse or partner.

"Hey, honey. What would you think of going to church more?"

"Hey, honey. We should find a better synagogue, don't you think?"

"Hey, honey. Do you think this volunteering opportunity would be a good fit?"

Just don't overuse the "Hey, honey" test. Apply it judiciously before making any big decisions.

The bottom line here is simple: faith is good, giving is good, volunteering is good. And while I'm not saying you *must* darken the doors of your place of worship for Sunday Mass or Shabbat service, I am saying that you should at least consider it. Legions of happy retirees have done it before you.

I know many of us have complicated relationships with religion, often stemming from our own families or childhoods. That's OK. Maybe you'll argue that the United States is a nation that was founded with a strict separation between church and state. I don't disagree. But that doesn't mean religion and religious principles weren't at the forefront of our forefathers' minds. Biblical concepts are woven throughout the Constitution, from a sense of justice to general welfare. "We the people" is a potent statement, and I believe that speaks to the power of community and our ability to come together to achieve great things.

If you're not currently a member of a faith-based community, and after reading this chapter, you are open to the idea, my advice is to start with baby steps. Finding the right place of worship is like any other worthwhile endeavor—it requires effort. The church down the street from you might not be right, but perhaps the one 10 miles away is. Go where you feel the most welcome and where the people around you have similar beliefs and values. If America's happiest retirees are any indication, you'll be glad you did.

Amen.

CHAPTER 8

Social Habits

CONNECT TO THRIVE

Social connection is crucial to survival. Most of us would inherently agree. Those who might find it a bit too "touchy-feely" would do well to summon the wisdom of kangaroos.

That's right. I just said the "wisdom of kangaroos." Don't @ me.

Kangaroo care is a method used in certain hospitals where an infant, naked except for a diaper and cap, is placed on the bare chest of the mother or father for several hours at a time. As you've probably deduced, the name is derived from the way an actual kangaroo holds its offspring, cuddled close in a marsupial pouch.

The technique was developed in Bogota, Colombia, in the late 1970s as a response to high death rates in premature infants. These tiny babies were dying at an alarming rate of 70 percent. The reported causes of death were infections and respiratory problems, though researchers posited a more nuanced theory: the preemies were really dying from a lack of attention and physical contact. The doctors believed the death rate of preterm infants could be drastically reduced if they were held close to the body of their mothers for large portions of the day.

They were right. These babies not only survived but thrived.[1]

In case the connection isn't obvious: Unhappy retirees survive. Happy retirees *thrive*. Hold me closer, tiny HROB.

In this chapter, I'll make a strong case that:

- **To be happy in retirement, you need *at least* three "CCs" (close connections), aka friendships.** More is great, too, but three seems to be the magic number. Unhappy retirees have 2.6 CCs. Happy retirees have 3.6.

- As we've seen with the Plateau Effect, more money early on leads to more happiness, but at a certain point, happiness plateaus. **There is no plateau when it comes to close social connections.** Quite simply, when it comes to close connections, more is better. Period.

- **Friends are a better happiness currency than money.** You heard me correctly. Money can't buy friends—but friends *can* buy happiness.

- **Happy retirees make a concerted effort to see their group of close social connections on a regular basis.** Once a year or even a few times a year doesn't cut it. Once you've got your three or more CCs, it's critical to make the effort to see them on average once a month.

- **Organized groups (and even semi- or loosely organized groups) create a powerful social epicenter to maintain social connectedness.** HROBs report belonging to at least one group. This could be a group organized around any activity, hobby, or interest under the sun that you can enjoy with other people. The kind of group and level of organization doesn't matter, only that you participate.

- **Travel with friends is another secret sauce of the HROB.** Respondents who reported that they "never" travel with friends are less likely to fall into the happy camp. However, just one trip per year—yes, only one—makes you twice as likely to land in the HROB camp. Start packing!

- **Many of the happiest retirees go to concerts.** This was one of my favorite findings from the latest research. There's a high correlation between loving music and being happy. HROBs know how to move and groove.

- **Socialization can happen anywhere.** We'll look at various ways to stay social, since, as the saying goes, different strokes for different folks.

And speaking of strokes: I'll also introduce you to Mary McCormick, a regular social butterfly who knows a thing or two about canoes.

But first: let's take a look at *why* socialization is so important to retirement happiness—and how it can literally keep you alive.

THREE IS THE MAGIC NUMBER—AND THERE'S NO PLATEAU FOR FRIENDS

You know I'm a research addict. Data is my friend, and it's telling me to expand my social circle.

My most recent study targeted individuals who were either within 10 years of retirement or in retirement already. Then, just like in the original study, I separated the respondents into the happy group and the unhappy group. Spoiler alert: those who had more close relationships were more likely to be in the happy camp.

Let's talk about *why* that is.

A recent study conducted by the health insurer Cigna confirmed an epidemic of "widespread loneliness, with nearly half of Americans reporting they feel alone, isolated, or left out at least some of the time."[2] Douglas Nemecek, MD, Cigna's chief medical officer for behavioral health, went so far as to say that "loneliness has the same impact on mortality as smoking fifteen cigarettes a day, making it even more dangerous than obesity."

There are two conclusions to be drawn here. One: don't smoke. Two: *have friends.*

In the new study, I asked retirees: How many people would you consider your "close" connections/friends? I defined "close" as people you would call to confide in about very good—or bad—personal news.

The results are clear (Figure 8.1): if your social network drops to 2 or fewer, you are 2.2 times more likely to be an unhappy

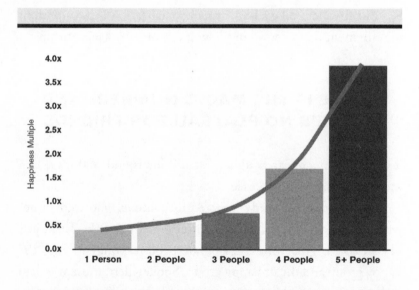

FIGURE 8.1 **Happiness Based on Close Connections/Friendships**

retiree. In average terms, UROBs had 2.6 CCs. HROBs had 3.6. *Three CCs (close connections) is the magic number.*

But why stop at three? Because here's the extra cool news: when it comes to friends, the more really is the merrier.

As you know by now, money does buy happiness—up to a certain point. After that, there are diminishing marginal returns. More money early on leads to more happiness, but then the impact begins to wane on overall happiness levels, hence the Plateau Effect.

However, quite the opposite is true with close social connections. *There's no plateau when it comes to close connections.* A greater number of close friends equals higher levels of happiness. Check out Figures 8.2 and 8.3.

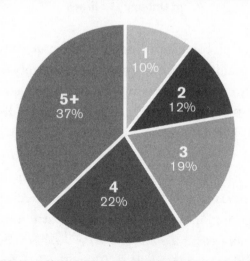

FIGURE 8.2 **Number of Close Connections/Friendships of Happy Retirees**

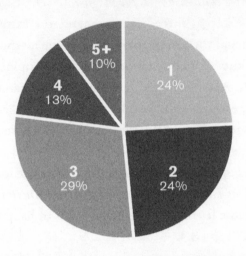

FIGURE 8.3 **Number of Close Connections/Friendships of Unhappy Retirees**

While you probably can't (and shouldn't) have 100 close friends to confide in, additional CCs beyond the mandatory three become exponentially more impactful to your retirement happiness. Social connectedness seems to have more of a compounding effect on your overall happiness than the accumulation of money past $500,000. Of course, this data doesn't diminish the positive impact that saving and investing have on retirement happiness. But these results make it clear that social connectedness has a similar, if not greater, impact—and once the party starts, it doesn't stop. *Close connections are an even better happiness currency than money.* And that's *me* saying that. The guy who's hosted *Money Matters* for well over a decade.

The prescription here is self-evident: prioritize forming and maintaining close social connections if you want to become and stay a happy retiree. Emphasis on *maintaining*. It goes without saying that you can't just decide you have three or more friends and then check it off the list. Friendship requires time, effort, and cultivation well beyond a message on Facebook.

Because I was curious exactly how much time and effort, I asked retirees how often they normally see or visit their circle of closest friends (Figure 8.4).

Once I crunched the data, the answer was about what I expected. Seeing friends more than once a week—and at least once a month—had the most positive impact on happiness in retirement. The key inflection point here is: *we need to see our close connections more than just once or a few times per year.*

The crucial importance of social connection has surfaced in my research over and over, not to mention in my personal experience

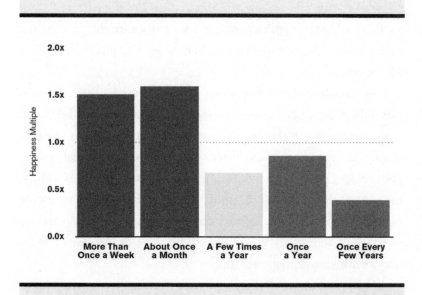

FIGURE 8.4 **How Often Do You See Your Close Connections?**

working with retirees for the past 20 years. It is abundantly evident that HROBs place an enormous emphasis on socialization: meaningful friendships and gathering in groups.

As a culture, we used to have more friends. According to my friend Dan Buettner, Americans had an average of three close friends in the 1980s. Today, with the prevalence of social media and digital "friends" (read: Facebook friends) and more people moving to the suburbs, Dan says that number has dropped to an average of 1.7.[3]

Good things come in threes—and the 1980s had it right all along. Now if they'd just bring back parachute pants and Madonna.

EAT, DRINK, AND BE
MARY MCCORMICK

Meet Mary McCormick, the perfect embodiment of a strong social spirit. Or, as I like to call her, "Eat, Drink, and Be Mary McCormick."

When Mary was in her fifties, she discovered a little community called Big Canoe about an hour-and-a-half north of Atlanta. Considered one of the South's premier mountain communities, Big Canoe has three lakes, three waterfalls, wildlife areas, parks, golf, tennis, pickleball, swimming, hiking trails, fishing, boating, fitness, spas, dining, and shopping. In short, it really embraces the *ings* (more on that in the next chapter). Big Canoe also has no shortage of activities geared toward kids—or, in the case of Mary McCormick, toward grandkids.

The joy of many of these activities is magnified by the opportunity to do them with others. Big Canoe offers walking groups, exercise groups, tennis groups, hiking groups, golf groups, dinner groups, poetry groups, chess groups, civics groups, charity groups—groups for anything under the gorgeous Georgia sun.

It's no surprise that Big Canoe is filled with happy retirees from metropolitan and suburban Atlanta. The website invites you to experience "Canoe Life," and that is exactly what the McCormicks decided to do. Mary and her husband—we'll call him Mr. Mary—bought a three-bedroom house in Big Canoe a couple of years before retirement. They used it on weekends and loved it so much that, after spending their whole adult lives in Atlanta, they decided to move into their Big Canoe house full-time after they retired.

It was a happy day when the McCormicks joined the 60 percent of Big Canoe residents who live full-time in the beautiful Blue Ridge Mountains. They are now officially my favorite HROLs: the happiest retirees on the lake.

As our frenemies at the *Wall Street Journal* reminded us, one of the great dangers of a post-career lifestyle is allowing social networks to decline.[4] On that point, at least, we agree. People like Mary seem to inherently know not to let that happen.

Even if you don't love your job—and if you're like four out of five Americans, you definitely don't—seeing coworkers every day can be an easy, low-stakes way to maintain friendships. Or at the very least to have acquaintances. There's a certain level of built-in social inertia that comes with the daily grind. As much as we may hate going to work, studies have shown that disconnecting from that office environment can lead to depression, anxiety, and other health problems.

Take, for example, a study by the Center for Retirement Research at Boston College that showed how retirement lowers the size and density of one's social network.[5] Alarmingly, the impact is especially large for women and college graduates. Smaller social networks and social isolation tend to reduce life satisfaction and impair physical and mental health.[6]

It is my professional opinion, backed up by data, that after you retire, your network shrinks and you have fewer soft-target opportunities to interact with people. You can (and must) manufacture your own hard targets. And if you're inspired by all this talk of targets: join an archery group. That's a great way to keep your eye on the prize.

GET YOUR GROUP ON

Ready for some tough love?

At this point in the chapter, you might be thinking, "I'm not like Mary McCormick, Wes. I'm not a social person. I hate canoes. I hate lakes. I hate mountains."

First, I'd encourage you to eliminate some of those "hates" from your vocabulary because you're sounding dangerously like a UROB.

Second, I'd ask you to reexamine what being "a social person" means. It's not something you're born with, like a blood type or a photographic memory. Being social isn't an either-or situation, where you either are or aren't for all eternity. Much like finding core pursuits, it's something you can build up to and work on, as you continue to grow and stretch yourself. You want to strengthen that human muscle of connection so that socializing becomes like oxygen: something you need to survive.

One proven tactic of the HROBs I've been lucky to work with is to stay active in social groups. These are exactly what they sound like: a group of people who meet up and do whatever they've decided to meet up and do. Some examples might be a church group, tennis team, running or hiking group, book club, civic engage-ment team, or neighborhood cleanup crew.

"Wait a minute," you say. "It's hard enough to make *one* new friend. Where am I supposed to find a whole horde of people?"

Here's the good news: *you only need one social epicenter to be a happy retiree.* My data showed that HROBs really only need to be part of one group to correlate to high levels of happiness. Belong-ing to just one group increased the likelihood of being an HROB by 1.7 times. Belonging to two to five groups increased the average likelihood of being an HROB by 2.1 times. But one is the magic number, so start there. Because here's the extra special bonus: so-cial groups often act as a social epicenter that can lead to *more* social connection and might even spawn tangential social groups.

Take, for example, the wonderfully well-known and popular group of brewpubs in Atlanta called Monday Night Brewing. The story behind MNB goes something like this: three guys met at church and formed a men's group. Among other things, they dis-covered they had a passion for brewing beer as a hobby. After a few years of casual brewing, the three friends opened a little brewery called Monday Night Brewing. Their love of hops and craft beer, typically with silly names, spawned an entire movement of brewer-ies (where you can buy draft beer, not food). They continue to be in business today, with multiple locations in the state of Georgia, and are leading the micro-brew revolution. One epicenter social group—in this case, church—led to a chain of breweries that con-tinues to foster a sense of community, incubating and hosting even more social groups.

Social groups beget social groups. It only takes one to get started—and you never know where that might lead.

For the record, I don't love craft beer. I'm more of a macro-brew guy. But I love this story.

ONE THING LEADS TO ANOTHER: THE CRAFT OF CONNECTION

Social groups—and being social in general—can take practice, work, and effort. Even the most social and extroverted humans must make a conscious effort to find and maintain friends with similar interests, especially once they don't have a ready-made network of colleagues and coworkers. On the upside: you no longer have to make idle conversation with Gary at the copy machine.

It's worth noting that you don't have to share the exact same beliefs, backgrounds, or even personality types as the people in your social network. Sometimes it's fun for a wallflower to hang out with the class clown, and vice versa. But I will say that finding friends who share your core pursuits can be a huge boon because it gives you a way to connect to what feels natural and, frankly, fun. For Mary, that happened to include a bunch of alpine activities. For the Monday Night Brewing guys, it was craft beer. For you, it could include gardening, gnome collecting, or golf.

Even if social connection is something you've neglected your entire life, it's not game over. Give yourself permission to focus on this part of the happy retiree equation, to invest real time and thought in different ways you can build your network and socialize with people in ways you enjoy.

And if you're still hitting a wall trying to imagine *how* to do these things, allow me to help. I've compiled a list of six potential ways to create social groups and find communities of friends. Feel free to try as many of these as you like. And if one of these catalyzes your own ideas for connecting, all the better.

1. **Traveling with friends, aka group excursions.** I love this one! Do it with your spouse and/or friends. There is nothing like exploring new locales and geographies to

forge lasting bonds. Think about your really good friends. If you're like me, the story of your friendship probably includes at least one trip you still fondly reminisce about. Even the most disastrous trips provide laughter in retrospect.

I asked my HROBs how often they traveled with friends, and the results didn't surprise me (Figure 8.5). This data clearly shows that traveling with friends is worth much more than the cost of your plane ticket. Doing so at least once a year seems to have a magically powerful impact. And traveling three or more times a year with friends more than *quadruples* your likelihood of retirement happiness. There's no substitute for it, so plan a trip!

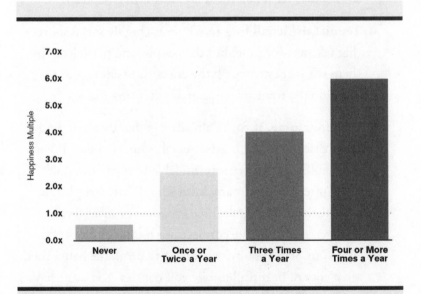

FIGURE 8.5 **Traveling with Friends**

2. **Faith-based and charitable activities.** Attend a new place of worship or a new group within it. If you skipped Chapter 7 in an anti-religious rage, now might be the time to flip back a few pages and read it for real.

3. **Civic groups.** Check out your local rotary club or your neighborhood civic association. There are also a rising number of neighborhood beautification groups that focus on activities like removing litter and graffiti, planting community gardens, and maintaining parks and green spaces.

4. **Exercise groups.** Cycling, running, hiking, walking, and even outdoor CrossFit-style bootcamp groups can provide a large potential network of interesting (not to mention fit) people. We'll talk more about this in Chapter 9.

5. **Tennis/pickleball league.** These are highly social sports that take a lot of time, but the people who participate in them swear they're worth the energy and effort, not to mention the tremendous exercise they provide.

6. **Golf foursome.** If you're already a golfer, then you know how perfectly suited it is for social connectedness. If you're not a golfer and it seems formidable to start now, don't be daunted! I know many folks who didn't start playing until their forties. Grab three friends—or meet three strangers—and let the connections on the green begin. And your new hobby doesn't have to break the bank; there are plenty of beautiful public golf courses. You don't have to play at Whistling Straits or Pine Valley—go to golfnow. com and find an affordable place to tee off. Case in point: there's a course near me called Bobby Jones Golf Course.

For slightly more than $20, I can play nine holes. Now that's a hole in one.

THE GIFT OF SONG: CONNECTING THROUGH MUSIC

Since the beginning of time, humans have loved music as a source of peace, healing, and happiness. It's a defining part of culture, from the clinking of two bones to Beethoven's Symphony to the Rolling Stones to Adele.

Music lovers, you're in luck: *many of the happiest retirees go to concerts.*[7] They recognize music for the gift it is—and they aren't afraid to jump up, jump up, and get down.

Live music can take many forms in our lives:

- Concerts

- Broadway/musicals

- Orchestra/symphony/opera

- Playing music by yourself or with other people

- Karaoke

According to a recent study out of London, experiencing live music may be the key to a longer lifespan.[8] (Somebody should tell the tortoises.) This synced up with the results from my own research. I must say I was surprised to see how many HROBs raved about going to concerts and shows. I think happy retirees realize live music accomplishes two things at once: lets them revel in a core pursuit, while also connecting with others who love the same music they do.

Juan and Carla Gonzales are a couple of HROBs who love music so much they moved to Nashville. They decided that in retirement they wanted to spend more time in a place that had a tremendous amount of access to live music—and they found it! Now on any given night, they can catch some of the greatest names in folk and country music.

Even if you don't have an organic interest in music, you can cultivate one. It's easy to listen to different musical genres at home and see what you love. You might even expand your horizons by getting friends to send you some of their favorite tunes. If you want another potential group activity, try this: form a music club with friends in which you share and listen to each other's music.

Before you know it, it'll be time for a field trip. It doesn't matter if it's the symphony, a pop concert with your kids or grandkids, a Chris Stapleton concert, a jazz festival, or a good ole rock-and-roll show put on by the Eagles. It's the act of getting out and enjoying music with others that will make your heart sing.

DREAM VACATION MEETS DREAM HOME

I want to paddle back to (Eat, Drink, and Be) Mary McCormick for a moment. You'll recall that Mary and her husband were able to buy a vacation home in Big Canoe a few years before retirement, which then became their main home after they retired. If you can afford it, it's a great idea to have a home in a vacation-oriented destination. Whether it's your primary or secondary home, there's no better incentive for your kids and your grandkids to come visit you.

As a matter of fact, that was one of the reasons *why* Mary and Mr. Mary made Big Canoe their full-time home. When they still lived in Atlanta, they noticed their adult kids visited them more up in the mountains. Although the McCormicks' adult kids can't afford a second home, they can and do bring the little ones to visit grandma and grandpa up in the Blue Ridge Mountains. It's not only a mini vacation spot for the entire family: it's a pleasant way to stay connected to each other.

I'll tell you another story. In the early days of Capital Investment Advisors, a client sent a letter to one of my fellow financial advisors, Curt Klein. Some years before, Curt had advised the client, Paula, to buy a house down on the beach in the Florida Panhandle. Included with the letter was a picture of her in a beach chair.

"Thank you so much for getting me to do this!" Paula wrote. "I've been enjoying this paradise for the last 15 years."

Not only did this earn her a new nickname—Paradise Paula—it cemented in my mind the fact that true value does not have dollar signs attached. Why had this decision turned out to be such a success for Paula? Was it the equity she made in the housing market? Not really. I mean, sure, the value had increased, but a house in that area has a lot of expensive upkeep costs. Despite a solid ROI, that wasn't why Paula loved it. It was because she constantly had visitors—her children, her grandchildren, her friends. Just like Mary up in Big Canoe, Paula and her husband had been able to develop a strong social network that kept them engaged and entertained.

Investing in a property like this, whether it's at the beach, up in the mountains, or in some other fabulous locale, is fine from a financial perspective. But the real power in this kind of investment lies in creating a hub for meaningful and enjoyable socialization. A purchase that is potentially priceless.

If you can't afford a home in Lake Canoe or along the sandy white beaches of the Florida Panhandle, you can still make meaningful connections. It doesn't have to break the bank. Just as core pursuits weren't determined by finances, the same is true here. It's not about the money you have—it's about what you use your money for.

In other words, *socialization can happen anywhere*. The cost can be anything, from free to exorbitant. All that matters is that you work within your budget and comfort zone, not only to maintain social connections, but to create new ones.

MOAIS: MEETING FOR A COMMON PURPOSE

I can't say enough good things about legendary author and cultural rock star Dan Buettner.

In *Blue Zones*, Dan introduced Western readers to the Moais of Japan, "social support groups that form in order to provide varying support from social, financial, health, or spiritual interests."[9] The term Moai means "meeting for a common purpose" and originated in Okinawa, Japan.

Each Moai is essentially a small group of five companions who have each other's backs. They diligently stick together for decades and offer support in various ways. They also keep one another happy and entertained. This is a concept we're not so familiar with here in the United States, a country that prides itself on rugged individualism and independence. It's practically coded into our DNA, this belief that we have to pull ourselves up by our bootstraps and go it alone.

Can you guess where this is going?

Let's take a look at the life expectancy of Okinawans—and the Japanese, more generally—compared to Americans (Figure 8.6).

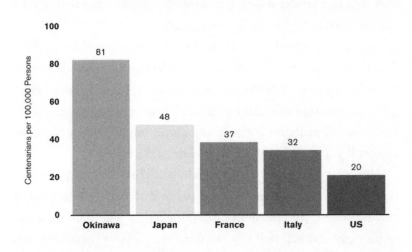

FIGURE 8.6 **Centenarian Prevalence by Country**
Source: "The Human Mortality Database," University of California, Berkeley
(USA), and Max Planck Institute for Demographic Research (Germany),
www.mortality.org or www.humanmortality.de (data downloaded in 2017);
Japan Ministry of Health Labour and Welfare 2017

There's no contest: Okinawans soar to the top of life expectancy, hands down.

No statistic exists in a vacuum. As Dan would be the first to attest, there are multiple nuanced variables that go into life expectancy calculations, which also encompass factors like diet.[10] Okinawans eat a primarily plant-based diet, whereas you never want to get in between a red-blooded American and a bone-in ribeye.

We'll go full-on bone and gristle in the next chapter when we talk about health. But for now: there's no denying that social connectedness correlates to longer life expectancy and happier lives.

You could have all the money in the world, but without close friends and a strong social epicenter, the chances of becoming or staying a happy retiree drop dramatically.

Go out and find your Moai. Make more than three friends. *Lots* more, if you can. Cultivate those relationships, and don't take them for granted. It might not be what we typically do in America when so much of our identity is bound up in being tough, stoic, and proud. But there's such a thing as too much cowboy bravado, at least if you're eyeing the HROB side of the street.

I'm not taking away your freedoms. What I'm saying is that you can be independent without being isolated, and connected without being codependent. You'll make it a whole lot easier to retire early *and* happy if you start bolstering your social network *now*. Chances are it'll make your retirement longer, too, by ensuring you're actually alive to enjoy it.

Think of Mary McCormick up in the Blue Ridge Mountains. Every Tuesday, she gets together with a small group of friends to play pickleball. Every Wednesday, they play canasta. And do you know what Mary, Ann, Muffy, Bridget, and Janet do every fall? They gather together in someone's cabin to watch Georgia football with their husbands.

Mary and her friends have the perfect Moai. Isn't it time you found yours?

CHAPTER 9

Health Habits

EAT, DRINK, AND HAVE A BALL

I'm not a health or fitness expert. There are plenty of books with specific advice on what you should eat, what you should *not* eat, and every type of exercise known to man. I'm here for one reason and one reason only: to help you retire early, happy, and healthy.

Emphasis on *healthy*. Because at the end of the day, HROBs make healthy choices.

John and Tiffany Ramos are a couple from Austin, Texas, proud citizens of the Lone Star State. Tiffany is 59. John, at 58, lovingly refers to himself as "Cougar Meat." He made that joke in the first few minutes of our introductory meeting. I found his cowboy twang so disarming, I couldn't help but laugh.

John and Tiff—or as I like to call them, Jiff—both juggle high-octane careers. John is a C-level executive at a healthcare company with an hour commute. Tiffany is the chief creative of an ad agency; since most of their campaigns are digital, it allows her to work from home. John and Tiff have three kids: two daughters in their early thirties, and a son, Rafael, who is disabled. He's in his early twenties and high functioning, but in all probability, they'll be taking care of him for the rest of his life.

When it comes to work, Tiff and John don't *hate* their jobs, but they don't love them either. They both want to be able to have more time with their children, especially their son. They'd also like to be more involved with their community, helping other families with disabled kids.

Like so many of the families I work with, they came to Capital because they wanted to know: *When can we stop working?*

That question is one of my favorites. It's why I write books. All the financial and lifestyle habits I've shared in these pages will help you create a happy, healthy, and joyful retirement.

But for me that's not good enough. It's of the utmost importance that I get you there *as soon as possible*, into an early retirement that is safe and secure. That's not an arbitrary goal. In some cases, it is literally life or death.

John and Tiff asked for my help in threading the needle. They wanted to figure out the exact date they could afford to shut off the paycheck valve and not run out of money. When I looked at Jiff's financials, I saw they were textbook HROBs: a million in savings, no mortgage, and a future pension from the healthcare company where John works. They'd both have Social Security in a few years, but in the meantime, they were eyeing early retirement.

"Y'all have nothing to worry about," I said. "You're doing everything right."

"Not *everything*," Tiff admitted. "We could both stand to be healthier. We eat takeout almost every night. We're obsessed with Salt Lick BBQ! And we never exercise."

"Not true," John said. "We play doubles tennis."

"We used to." Tiff's face fell. "Not anymore."

Only then did I realize there was something else going on. I noticed Tiffany's eyes were getting a little watery. And now that John's initial jolly demeanor had worn off, I saw something in his eyes, too. If you've ever experienced true grief, you know it when you see it.

"What's wrong, what's going on?" I asked.

"We just lost someone," Tiff blurted, clearly relieved to say it out loud. "One of our closest friends."

Tiff proceeded to tell me about Tanner, John's best friend from his college days at UT Austin. Tanner and his wife, Elena, were the other couple in those doubles tennis matches. But a few months earlier, Tanner had a heart attack while driving home from work. He was gone in the blink of an eye.

I gave my condolences to Jiff, and they graciously accepted them.

"He was only 58," Tiff said tearfully. "Fit as a fiddle. Or at least, he used to be."

John cleared his throat. "Maybe not as fit as we thought. Elena said that Tanner's diet had been kind of a disaster for years, and he had some health problems he wasn't talking about. His doctor said he was prediabetic. The reality is that tennis every once in a while with them was the only exercise any of us got."

John and Tiff confessed that losing Tanner was one of the main catalysts in coming to see me. It was so sudden—and so heartbreaking—it made them reevaluate the path they were on.

"It reminded us life is short," John said. "Only God knows when we're going to go. In the meantime, we want to spend as much quality time with our kids and friends as possible. We want to have time to enjoy the fruits of our labor. And we *don't* want to spend a single minute longer than we have to pushing paper at our jobs."

"It also reminded us we have to stay healthy," Tiff added. "We owe it to ourselves and our children. Especially Raf, who needs us to be at our best. Even if we don't know exactly when we're going to go, we do have control over some things. And if we want to stay healthy and well during our golden years, we know we better start now."

I couldn't agree more.

I'm going to shoot straight with you: it's not uncommon for retirees to indulge in unhealthy habits. Especially UROBs. They sit around, watch too much Netflix, overeat, and overdrink. Some even smoke, despite the fact that literally everyone in America over the age of three knows that smoking cigarettes is like playing Russian roulette with your lungs. These choices and behaviors are disastrous to physical health, and they can bleed over into emotional health, too, creating the perfect cocktail for depression.

Remember "Ironic," that Alanis Morissette song? The lyrics start out: "An old man turned 98. He won the lottery . . . and died the next day." It's not hard to draw the parallel. I think a lot about the guy who waited and waited and waited to retire . . . and died the next week. Isn't it ironic?

This is exactly why I launched the Retire Sooner podcast. I want you to retire as soon as makes sense for you. But if you are unhealthy, that's not great, either. All the wealth in the world means nothing if you're knocking on death's door.

But there is hope. HROBs take their health seriously, and their fitness, food, and drink habits paint a very different portrait than that of their unhappy counterparts. In this chapter, we'll discuss many healthy habits shared by the happiest retirees, including:

- **Happy retirees are fans of the "*ing*s."** These are low-cost forms of exercise like walking, swimming, biking, and hiking. That doesn't mean HROBs are out running marathons every few months. But it *does* mean they don't succumb every night to those other treacherous *ing*s: sitting and watching HBO.

- **Happy retirees gravitate toward a healthy diet.** In fact, you are three times more likely to be a happy retiree if you follow the Mediterranean diet. Vegetarians, and even those who prefer a "meat and potatoes diet," don't fare too badly, either. Of course there's no perfect happy retiree diet, but HROBs take their food intake seriously, and generally stay away from fast food.

- **Happy retirees report white wine and gin as their favorite alcoholic choices.** That's right: you don't have to be a teetotaler. Go grab a bottle of nice gin, Campari, and sweet vermouth, and make yourself a Negroni. Better yet, let Stanley Tucci show you how.[1]

WHEN TENNIS MET GOLF: A LOVE STORY

Being active is vitally important—and that's not an idle word choice. If you want to stay vital, a word that shares a Latin root with the word *alive*, you must incorporate some kind of exercise into your life.

The happiest retirees are active. They make exercise a staple of their weekly schedule, if not their daily routine. HROBs love the *ing*s, high-impact activities such as:

- Walking
- Hiking
- Biking
- Jogging
- Running
- Swimming

Most of the *ing*s can be done at or around your home for free. You might need a pool to go swimming, though, unless your bathtub is exceptionally large.

Then there are the racquet sports, tennis and badminton. I'm not exaggerating when I say these sports might unlock the secrets of the death-defying Galapagos tortoise. A Danish study followed more than 8,000 people over a period of 25 years to determine which physical activities most affected longevity when compared to a sedentary lifestyle.[2] What they found was remarkable: tennis added *9.7 years* to life expectancy. Badminton tacked on 6.2 years. The runners-up were soccer (4.7 years), cycling (3.7), swimming (3.4), jogging (3.2), and calisthenics (3.1).

For all you reluctant gym rats: the least beneficial form of exercise was working out at the gym, which added only 1.5 years to life expectancy. Give yourself permission to cancel that gym membership—as long as you grab a tennis racquet or heartily engage in some *ing*s. As the Danish would say, you deserve a *langt liv*.

Why is tennis so good for you? The researchers aren't sure, but they have a couple of theories.[3] First, tennis and other racquet sports are a form of interval training, which means they consist of short bursts of high-intensity activity as opposed to a protracted period of steady exertion.

Second—and perhaps more significant—racquet sports require two or more people. As a result, these games foster regular social interaction that, as we saw in the last chapter, is proven to support the mental and physical health of older people. A long solo bike ride is healthy. A shorter weekly bike ride with a group might be healthier.

I have a soft spot for tennis because my mom, a total HROB, is an avid player. She lives for tennis and her tennis friends. For her sixtieth birthday, her entire tennis team came to her house in Westchester, Pennsylvania, and held a de facto awards ceremony. They gave out awards for Biggest Grunter, Most Intense, Sorest

Loser, Best Winner, Best High-Fiver, and even Best Tennis Outfit. Those ladies had a blast.

It should be said that tennis is not actually a magical elixir. The study doesn't definitively prove that tennis leads to longevity; many of the participants who played tennis were just healthier, more active people in general. But at the very least, this data offers more proof that life is for the living, and that staying active, both physically and socially, adds quality to our years, regardless of their number.

Which brings us, naturally, to golf.

I've talked about golf a lot, so you know my bias. But I didn't start out that way. My father hated golf for some reason, and because of that, I grew up thinking it was a ridiculous sport. If Dad didn't want to attend a social event, his default excuse was, "Oh, I've got a golf lesson that day," delivered with a heaping dose of sarcasm. Subtext: I'd rather do anything else on earth than go to that luncheon.

My opinion of golf changed after writing my first book, mostly because I realized how enjoyable the game can be. Getting some exercise in the sun with my buddies, hitting a ball, and sipping an ice-cold brew? They actually let adults do this?

The catch-22 is that golf is one of those things that gets a lot more difficult to start the longer you wait. If you've never cooked a day in your life, you could still become a phenomenal chef starting at age 70, 80, or 90. When it comes to mastery in the kitchen, age is irrelevant. Golf, on the other hand, is different. It's a lot easier to pick up golf as a 10-year-old than as a 70-year-old.

That said, I know plenty of people who started golf in their forties. The *Wall Street Journal* wrote a piece about a guy who didn't start playing until he was 50 and shot his age at 72.[4] These late-bloomer golfers now enjoy the game immensely, despite not starting as a baby like prodigy Tiger Woods. (I'm not kidding—the guy was six months old.[5])

Long story short: starting golf at an older age is not impossible. But if you're thinking of picking up a club, do it soon, because it gets more difficult the longer you wait. Golf checks multiple boxes at once: it's a core pursuit, a physical activity, and a way to be social.

There's not really a wrong way to be active. In my mid-forties, I'm constantly coaching my kids in various sports or chasing them around the house. My wife and I try to *ing* whenever we can, even when all we have time for is walk*ing* the dogs. And I've always got my clubs in the back of my car.

Tennis, golf, pickleball: they're all relatively inexpensive pastimes that are highly social, involving either two or four people. It's never too late to have a ball.

A Retiree's Best Friend

Tell you a secret: I'm currently recording these words while on a walk with my two canine buddies, Josie and Kodie.

Anyone who has a dog can attest that they're good for you. A recent *Time* magazine article published the facts and figures to back it up.[6] Studies have shown that dogs can lead to lower levels of stress; they've also been found to decrease the risk of asthma in children and have been linked to lower blood pressure.

Perhaps best of all, dog owners are more active than your average person. As opposed to sitting on the couch, trying to summon your better angels, and forcing yourself to take a walk, you suddenly have an urgent reminder in the form of a lovable furball staring up at you with his leash in his mouth. Who can say no to that?

If you want a surefire way to be more active, have more fun, and make a lifelong friend, consider getting a dog. Your local shelter is full of animals who are looking for their forever home.

THE TRUTH ABOUT DIETING: EATING WELL CAN BE HEALTHY *AND* DELICIOUS

Real talk: none of us are as young as we used to be. As I ease into the soft hills and valleys of my mid-forties—metaphorically *and* physiologically—one thing my body has emphatically told me is that you can't jog your way out of a bad diet. Unless your name is Michael Phelps, it's best not to swing by the diner for "three sandwiches of fried eggs, cheese, lettuce, tomato, fried onions and mayonnaise; add one omelet, a bowl of grits and three slices of French toast with powdered sugar; then wash down with three chocolate chip pancakes."[7] Those 10,000 calories per day don't work so well when you're not training for the Olympics.

Our data shows that *happy retirees love a health-conscious diet, while unhappy retirees have a greater propensity toward less healthy options that include fast food.*[8] But that doesn't mean happy retirees don't enjoy eating. HROBs prioritize healthy food. Many observe what's commonly referred to as "the Mediterranean diet," which is a fancy way of saying they consume lots of fish, poultry, vegetables, fruits, whole grains, healthy fats, beans, and eggs, while limiting their intake of overprocessed junk food.

In other words, it's nothing crazy. It's a way to eat healthy without setting yourself up for the kind of failure (and hunger pains) we've all experienced when cycling through fads, fasting, and deprivation diets. If you've ever Googled "banana" to find the calorie count, you know what I mean.

That said, the happiest retirees also know how to treat themselves on special occasions. Over years of collecting data on HROBs, I've learned they love indulging once in a while on a nice juicy steak. Steak gets a bad rap in today's health-obsessed culture, but Ruth Chris Steak House actually shows up over and over again as an HROB go-to spot.

The Mediterranean diet is just one option. The overarching theme is that clean eating is key. You want to make a conscious effort toward a healthy diet, while reducing—or better yet, avoiding—the bad stuff like fast food. HROBs aren't happy because they eat Mediterranean, and UROBs aren't *un*happy because they hit the drive-through at Mickey D's. But their food choices reflect their attitude toward maintaining their own health. We should all be making cleaner, healthier choices in the foods we eat, not only for our body's longevity, but because it reflects the focus and discipline we'll need to take care of ourselves in retirement.

If you know your diet needs improvement, I might even nudge you toward braving the kitchen now and then to rustle up some dinner. You don't have to be a great cook, but preparing your own meals is a great way to know exactly what's in the food you're eating.

Who knows? Maybe you'll discover a previously untapped passion for cooking and pick up a new core pursuit along the way. My team and I dream about someday writing *You Can Cook Better Than You Think*, the Wes Moss cookbook. What a triumph it would be to finally wipe that smug look off my brothers' faces as they realize they aren't the true Anthony Bourdains of the family. Not that their "bad cook" jokes bother me. Who cares what they think? My wife loves my cooking.

Unless she's just being nice.

The truth is that for most of my life I thought the formula for good health was 90 percent exercise, 10 percent diet. But as we get older, we realize we can't fight a bad diet no matter how much we hit the treadmill at the gym. You can't fuel a car with junk and expect it to keep running like a clean, mean fighting machine.

Once I finally learned how to curb my bad eating habits, it made a dramatic impact on my life from a health perspective. My blood pressure went down by 20 percent. I dropped 15 to 20 pounds. My joints felt better, my energy levels skyrocketed, and my skin cleared up. It was a true transformation that came from diet versus just exercise.

What specifically did I eat? I took a month-long challenge and did the Whole30, an elimination diet that isn't too dissimilar from the Mediterranean diet.[9] The goal of Whole30 is to eat whole foods and eliminate the unhealthy stuff most of us eat without thinking twice: sugar, empty carbohydrates, processed foods. It's also a chance to temporarily eliminate certain foods that affect some metabolisms and not others: legumes, grains, etc. After 30 days, you start to gradually reintroduce foods, seeing how you feel, and then use that information to achieve long-term "food freedom."

Whole30 isn't for everyone. It's fairly restrictive, and it's not meant to be observed forever. If it works the way it's supposed to, you learn which foods your body responds to favorably and which foods it doesn't. After those 30 days, I took what I had learned and applied it to a diet that was more sustainable long term. I'm forever grateful for Whole30: it really did set me on the path of knowing how to eat in a healthier way.

These days one of my secret weapons with a house full of four kids is a service called Atlanta Meal Prep.[10] I can order precooked meals and not resort to a bucket of fried chicken when I need something quick. There is different pricing depending on the number of meals you want that week, and they all adhere to your specific dietary needs. I love it.

For those of you clutching your chocolate bars close to your chest: it's OK to indulge on occasion. Chocolate has been found to lower blood pressure, and hot cocoa can boost the blood supply to your brain and increase memory. When it comes to chocolate, the darker the better—leave the milk for the cows.

PROHIBITION IS OVER: HAVE A DRINK

If you're like most Americans, you know at least one alcoholic, whether it's Uncle Jim Bob having way too many beers at Christmas dinner or that college friend who kept on drinking like she did in college . . . for the next 30 years.

You might be thinking, "Uh-oh. I better go empty out the liquor cabinet because Wes is going to tell me I have to be a teetotaler to be happy."

My friend, do I have news for you!

Plenty of happy retirees drink. In my last study, I found that retirees who had one or two drinks per day were just as happy as those who had zero drinks per day. So assuming there isn't some underlying issue or addiction à la Uncle Jim Bob, you have my blessing to imbibe. And if you're a nondrinker, you have my blessing to drink Shirley Temples. You can be happy either way.

For what it's worth, one consistent finding is that *happy retirees love to drink white wine and gin.* (Bonus: if you're looking for a side hustle, consider becoming a *gin*tern.[11]) Champagne is also welcome. One to three glasses of bubbly per week can ward off dementia and memory loss, according to a 2013 British study.[12] Something in champagne seems to encourage healthy levels of certain brain proteins that tend to deplete with age.

And if you're not a fan of pinot grigio but love a nice pinot noir: I've got you covered. Red wine has long been known to have several health benefits, including supporting your good cholesterol levels. But get this: the resveratrol in one glass of red wine can improve heart and muscle strength as much as an hour in the gym.

Resveratrol is also found in some fruits and nuts. But who cares? It's in red wine.

Be Transcendent:
The Health Benefits of Meditation

In the not-so-distant past, the idea of meditation conjured up images of Buddhist monks sitting cross-legged in their bright saffron-dyed robes. Today, East meets West as meditation (and mindfulness, its kissing cousin) has been widely embraced by doctors and scientists for its many health benefits.

Healthline recently aggregated dozens of studies and findings on meditation, highlighting 12 science-based benefits of meditation.[13] These range from stress reduction and decreased blood pressure to mental clarity, less pain, and a more positive outlook on life.

I've recently started watching YouTube videos on transcendental meditation and am trying to do some TM myself. I'm a long way off from being a guru, but I've already noticed positive results. For me, meditation is a way to quiet down all the noise in my brain and gain back some peace of mind. Not always easy to do in a house with four boys, two dogs, and the ever-present goal of creating a million extra years of retirement here in the United States.

MARKING THE MAP:
STAYING HEALTHY IN THE USA

I recently received an email from a man we'll call Marcus Band. Marcus and his wife, Kayla, met with me a few years ago, back when they were planning their retirement. Since then, they've been clients of my colleagues at Capital.

The Bands recently tuned into my Retire Sooner podcast where they heard me talking about my new book on retiring healthy and happy. "We are happy retirees, Wes," Marcus wrote. "Kayla and I believe that family, friends, eating well, daily exercise, and maintaining an active lifestyle have been the key to our great retirement success. Kayla is an excellent cook and focuses on preparing healthy meals for us every day. And no matter where we are, we make exercise a top priority every day, which includes doing resistance training, aerobics, and even yoga!"

Marcus wasn't kidding about being an HROB success story. He went on to say that he and Kayla are socially active; they see friends regularly and belong to social clubs centered on interests, like motorcycle riding and wine club groups. They spend time almost daily, either in person or virtually, with their three children and seven grandchildren. They have a motorhome they love and use it to travel, exploring this beautiful country of ours.

But my favorite part of the Bands' story was the picture Marcus sent of Kayla standing beside a magnetic map of the United States affixed to the back of their motorhome (Figure 9.1). Twenty-two states boasted colorful magnets. "Our goal is to visit every state in the nation over the next few years," Marcus wrote. "Twenty-eight to go. And yes, we've gotten some strange looks from people as they watched these two 'old people' drag out dumbbells and resistance bands to start working out at the campsite. But we believe

FIGURE 9.1 **The Bands Traverse America**

keeping our bodies, minds, and spirits strong is how we are going to live a long and meaningful life."

I couldn't have said it better myself.

As for Tiffany and John, the famous Jiff? They're doing great. John has started jogging in the mornings before work, and Tiffany just bought a Peloton for the basement. Now when she breaks for lunch, Tiff gets in some revs before grabbing a nutritious salad. She and John still treat themselves to Salt Lick BBQ on occasion—their son Raf loves it—but only as a special treat. They recently subscribed to an ingredient-and-recipe meal kit service, and Tiff is learning to cook. To her surprise, now that she's got a recipe to follow and the exact ingredients and quantities she needs, she enjoys it.

My prediction? Not only will Jiff retire early, they're soon to embark on the healthiest, happiest, sweetest time of their lives. Now that's a recipe worth following.

CHAPTER 10

Home Habits

LIVE MORTGAGE FREE

It's a rare week when someone doesn't ask me about mortgages. Clients, radio callers, even friends—it seems like every single person wonders if, how, and when they should pay theirs off. There's a lot of conflicting information out there, and nobody wants to get it wrong.

A mortgage is often the biggest expense we take on in our lifetimes. We spend more money buying a house than we do sending our kids to college. Unless you can buy your home outright, which 99.95 percent of Americans can't afford to do, you end up with a mortgage, which is a pretty hefty chunk of debt.

Banks set up mortgages a long time ago under fairly nefarious terms, with long payment schedules that last 15, 30, even 40 years. In the classic 30-year mortgage, you basically end up paying for the house *twice* because of the interest. You also spread out your biggest payment over multiple decades.

While you have a mortgage, it's the bill that's always there, always lingering. It's a constant, mind-numbing refrain that sticks in your head worse than an Alanis Morissette song. *Gotta pay the mortgage. Gotta pay the mortgage.* It's your biggest single monthly outlay, and it follows you around relentlessly. No wonder there's so much joy and comfort and happiness waiting just over the rainbow, once that mortgage is a thing of the past.

If you can afford to pay off your mortgage, do it. That's the financial and lifestyle habit at the heart of this chapter. One irrefutable thing I've learned from my research over the years is that, regardless of your interest rate and the cost, getting rid of your mortgage by the time you retire is a powerful indicator of happiness.

In this chapter, we'll look at several key home habits of the happiest retirees, including:

- **HROBs pay off their mortgages.** The happiest retirees have eliminated—or are very close to eliminating—their mortgage payments. We'll discuss several important factors to consider when paying off your mortgage, including whether or not you can safely do so, using the One-Third Rule.

- **Happy retirees live in nice houses, but not McMansions.** It's OK to be comfortable. It's less OK to have exotic zebras grazing on the 400-acre ecofarm you call home.

- **The happiest retirees know that neighborhoods and networks are more important than their four walls.** It can be tempting to want to move to greener pastures. But sometimes, when you've spent years cultivating your community, the best nest might just be the one you've been roosting in all along.

- **HROBs don't downsize.** This is a new habit gleaned from my most recent study. HROBs don't downsize into a smaller place, mainly because they anticipate their kids and grandkids will be coming home to visit.

This chapter is meant to arm you with the right strategies to really get rolling. Hear that horn honking outside? That's me, cruising up to the curb, ready to drive you to the happiest retiree block party. How do we get there? By helping you pay off your mortgage sooner than you thought.

SHOULD I PAY OFF MY MORTGAGE? THE ONE-THIRD RULE

To pay or not to pay. That is the question. It's the question Hamlet would have asked if he'd survived long enough to buy his own castle in Denmark—and the question that still divides financial planners today.

Some money pros think you are better off investing your surplus money rather than using it to pay off or pay down your mortgage. They believe you will get a larger net return by continuing to pay interest on your house while investing leftover resources and earning a higher return in the stock market. Instead of using $100,000 to pay off a 4 percent mortgage, they'll tell you to invest it in the market where you could see a return of, say, 8 percent. The result: a net 4 percent gain of $4,000.

Look, I get it. In theory, it makes sense. But last time I checked, we live in the real world, and often this strategy fails the real-world test. In the real world, the market could be flat for a decade, as it was in the 2000s, or it could crash and burn just before you need to cash in.

For me, paying off your mortgage takes out the guesswork. It's a surefire thing. Once that prodigious debt is off your shoulders, no one gets to take a 4 percent bite out of your joy.

I've thrown a lot of charts and graphs at you in this book, and you've gamely caught every pass. The one in Figure 10.1 is a classic. Have you ever seen such clean, beautiful stairsteps? As the years to pay off the mortgage go down, happiness levels go up, smooth and simple.

The happiest retirees report that there is a real sense of peace and serenity that comes from knowing you own your house free and clear. It just feels good as you enter a new phase of life. I call this the *Ahhhh* factor. When you relieve yourself of this financial and psychological burden, you can breathe a giant sigh of relief. Eliminating a house payment also dramatically lowers your monthly retirement living expenses, thus taking pressure off your nest egg and other sources of monthly income. Talk about a stress reliever!

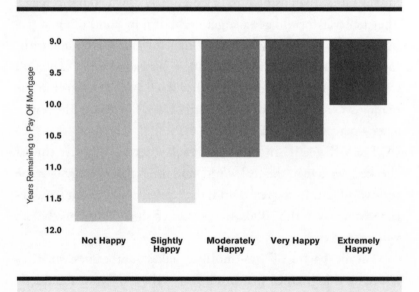

FIGURE 10.1 **Years Until Mortgage Is Paid Off**

There's no one-size-fits-all solution when it comes to eliminating your mortgage. People have different circumstances, savings, and tolerance for risk. But if there's one rule I've seen liberate thousands of retirees and pre-retirees, catapulting them toward happiness, it's the One-Third Rule. *If you can pay off your mortgage using no more than one-third of your nonretirement savings, do it.*

Let's say you have $300,000 in savings and your mortgage is $90,000. You have my blessing to take one-third of your after-tax money and pay it off. Boom! Done.

If you have $1 million in your IRA or 401(k) but only $100,000 in after-tax, and you have a $300,000 mortgage: do not pass go. The ratio doesn't work because almost all of that is retirement money.

One of the most common questions I get is, "Do I pay off my mortgage with my retirement fund? I've got $400,000 in my 401(k) and my mortgage is $200,000. Shouldn't I just pay it off?"

The answer is: absolutely not.

Let's take a run at this from a slightly different perspective. If you're still working and making, say, $100,000, and then you pull out another $200,000, all of a sudden, your income is $300,000. Your tax bracket goes through the roof. Now you've just had to pay a huge tax bill in order to pay off the mortgage. It creates a tax tsunami—and you'll want to run for the hills.

You will almost never want to use retirement-account money—IRAs, 401(k)s—to pay off a mortgage. Remember, paying off your mortgage is about creating peace of mind. Tapping your pretax retirement nest egg won't do that. Reducing your hard-earned retirement reserves undercuts your future security by decreasing actual cash and future income earnings on that account. (You can access those funds in a more tax-efficient way—we'll talk about that in Chapter 11.)

The reason I like the One-Third Rule is that it makes things cut and dry. Can you pay off your mortgage and still have at least two-thirds of your after-tax money left? Excellent. Take the plunge. And if you can't? Time for a different approach.

If the One-Third Rule isn't in play for you, your next best option might be the Extra Payment Plan. This is where you either pay an additional amount of principal with each monthly payment, or make 13 mortgage payments per year instead of 12. In fact, most happy retirees who have paid off their mortgages did so by paying more than the minimum monthly payment each month over several years. In my experience, about 70 percent of retirees who are mortgage-free used this method to reach that goal.[1]

Here's an example of how it might work. Let's say you just bought a house last year. Welcome home! I'll bring a bottle of gin as a housewarming gift.

If you have just started a 30-year mortgage of $250,000 at 5 percent interest, your scheduled monthly payment will be $1,342. Adding $300 per month to that payment will slice nine years and four months off the life of the loan—and save $79,684 in interest (Figure 10.2).

You read that right. If you make an additional mortgage payment of just $300 a month—the price of two nice steak dinners—you shave nearly a *decade* off a 30-year mortgage. That's pretty impressive.

If a monthly payment just isn't doable, you might consider saving up to make an extra mortgage payment every year. You could structure your payment plan so that you pay 50 percent of your monthly obligation every two weeks. That's a painless way to make an extra month's payment every 12 months.

Or maybe you get a sudden windfall of cash after your wealthy Aunt Bertha passes away. You thought the woman hated your guts,

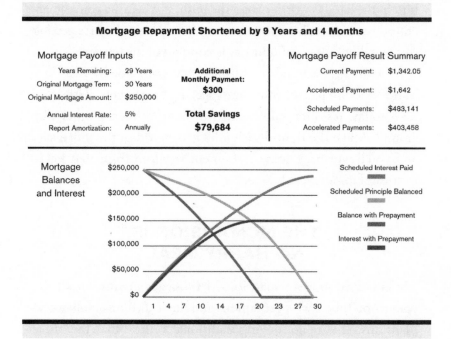

FIGURE 10.2 **Early Mortgage Payoff**

but it turns out you were her favorite—and the lawyer of her estate calls to tell you just how much her affections were worth. If you can pay off your mortgage in a big chunk and still stay financially secure, do it. You just want to make a solid plan so that you're either paid off or mostly paid off by the time you retire. If you're 58 and you're retiring at 65, let's get a plan in place to pay your house off over the next five to eight years.

As I was writing this chapter, I met a couple who was facing the usual mortgage dilemma. We'll call them Mitch and Morgan Mortimer. Morgan said to me, "Our mortgage is only 2.85 percent. I know we shouldn't pay it off. We should invest it somewhere else because our money should be growing more than that."

To which I replied, "In theory, you're right. But I'm actually a big advocate for getting rid of the mortgage. Not only because a bird in the hand is worth two in the bush, but because you're guaranteed to save the 2.85 percent year after year. And you're getting this wonderful peace of mind by getting rid of the burden."

I won't beat around the bush. If you can abide by the One-Third Rule and pay off your mortgage, do it tomorrow. Better yet: do it today. It's often said a house owns you, not the other way around. Make the right decision by getting rid of the mortgage, and you'll win back some retirement freedom from that fickle mistress, Home Sweet Home.

THE MCMANSION IS NO HAPPY MEAL

My kids love modern mansions. I think it's because of all the young YouTubers who get famous and buy ridiculous Hollywood mansions. They're not buying traditional Tudors; they buy these big modern white houses with gigantic glass windows and 12 balconies, and then they turn the interior into a leisure center with a movie theater, bowling alley, golf simulator, and oxygen bar.

Spoiler alert: there are no happy retirees hiding behind those floor-to-ceiling glass windows. *HROBs live in nice houses, but not McMansions.*

In one of my first retirement research studies conducted back in 2013, the average HROB home value came out to around $355,000. I was amazed that even the happiest retirees didn't have home values that exceeded $400,000 (on average).

Of course, real estate prices have jumped so dramatically, that number needs a face-lift. While many tried-and-true HROB statistics like income, spending, and liquid net worth still hold water, HROB home values have to be adjusted for 2021's unprecedented housing market inflation. You could say the seeds were sown back in 2007 and 2008, when the mortgage bust led to a massive underbuilding of new homes—meaning there weren't enough to meet demand when the current "work from anywhere" mega trend hit, with millions of Americans favoring home offices.

According to the Case-Shiller US National Home Price Index,[2] there was a staggering 65 percent increase in home values from 2013 to 2020. Using that number as a baseline, I've increased the HROB's average home value by 65 percent to get today's value of $585,000. A pretty impressive spike when you consider all an HROB had to do to their home was simply stay in it!

Staycations Just Don't Work

Staying in your home long term is a good HROB move. Staying in your home and calling it a vacation? Not so good. After 2020, we've all had enough staycations to last a lifetime. But long before COVID-19 locked the world down and massively restricted travel, my happy retiree research showed that no matter what cute clever name you stick on it, staying in your home does *not* count as a vacation. If you're not getting away, you're not actually flipping your mindset to be somewhere else.

According to my data, if staycations were a person's most common form of vacation, they were 2.5 times more likely to land in the unhappy camp. Happy retirees do not stay cooped up at home.

Yes, some HROBs do have modest vacation homes. I'm not saying you can't stay in your vacation home and still be happy. We'll talk about that next. Just know that a staycation isn't a long-term substitute for the real thing. Sometimes you have to get away to get happy.

SHOULD WE GET A SECOND HOUSE?

I get this question all the time.

"We live in Charlotte. Should we get a place in Hilton Head?"

"We live in Atlanta. Should we get a place down in the Florida Panhandle?"

Couples want to know if they can afford to get a place somewhere in the mountains or on a lake that's not going to be dramatically expensive.

If you want to have a second home somewhere magical, you're certainly not alone. You may be daydreaming about buying a place in St. Augustine, Florida, one of America's most wonderful historic cities. Or getting a ski condo up in Park City, Utah. Or purchasing a rustic ranch under the big sky in Jackson Hole, Wyoming. These all sound great.

But whenever people ask me about a second home, I first steer them back to the Holy Grail of house habits: *have a plan to pay off your primary home mortgage first.*

Burning the mortgage leaves you more money to follow your dreams and passions, including the ones that inspire you to leave home. The money you've been sending to Bank of America on the first of the month is now yours to use as you wish. You could spend it on more vacations, hobbies, or charitable giving—or you can use it to buy that cabin in Bozeman, Montana that you've been coveting since 2003.

Once you get rid of the debt on your primary residence, I'm all for you getting a second place on the coast or up in the Blue Ridge Mountains. As long as you're not buying something too speculative, a vacation property can be a good investment, and it allows you to be flexible: even if you only keep it for a few years, you can ideally sell it for a similar or greater amount. If you can afford a second home, I think it's a great option.

And in case you were wondering, there is no discernible difference in happiness when it comes to where that second home is located. In a recent research study, I tested houses on the beach versus in the mountains versus on the lake in relation to retiree happiness, and there was no uptick or downtick for any location. But I will tell you, I see utter and pure enjoyment when families are able to have some sort of second home or getaway that they go to over and over again.

We live in a world of Airbnb where we can rent a place in any location at any time. That's great! I love Airbnb and have used it many times over the years. But what you don't normally hear about is just how much you love going back to that exact same Airbnb with the whole fam. Even if you find one you love, it'll probably be full next time you try to book it. Those places don't become a second home or a second community.

But when retirees have some sort of secondary family gathering place? There is something very powerful, even magical about having a family cottage or cabin or lake house, some shared location where you go to spend time on a recurring basis. It doesn't have to be fancy. What makes it special is that you are getting away *together*.

If you can afford to have someplace for the family to go as a group, very rarely will you regret it. One caveat, though: if you've got little kids, I can say from personal experience that it's hard to utilize a second place because kids tend to get busy with school and sports and ballet and all of the activities they have. I've seen younger couples get frustrated when they've invested in a second home and then their kids' schedules are too complicated for them to actually use it. However, as parents get a little older and their kids get a little more independent, a vacation home can be a wonderful gift to yourselves. The happiest retirees would rather have one modest home and a second beloved cabin for family getaways than one giant modern mansion.

Which brings me to my next topic.

Some retirees aren't interested in a vacation home, but they are very much interested in getting a fresh start. Moving out of their current home into a brand-new one can seem like a magic elixir, a way to push the reset button on their lives. When housing markets are hot, relocating is extra tantalizing; a strong seller's market dangles a most tempting carrot.

The truth, however, is that these decisions are about a lot more than dollars and cents.

To illustrate why that's true, I'm going to pass the mic to Tidy-Up Tessa.

TIDY-UP TESSA: IT'S ALL ABOUT THE NEIGHBORHOOD

Tessa was a family friend. She'd lived in her home for many years, and happily so. But she had recently lost her husband, and in the wake of his death, she was thinking of downsizing. She wondered if a new home might help her move through her grief and into this new phase of her life.

As we talked, Tessa was very emotional. She truly loved her home, but it was hard for her to imagine staying in a house she'd shared with her husband for the last 30 years now that he was gone.

"Can you tell me what you love about where you live?" I asked.

Tessa's whole face lit up. "Well, I love my neighborhood. There's a group of women in our late fifties and early sixties—we have a book club and get together every week and drink wine. It's a lot of fun. My neighbor Jack across the street has become a good friend, and he's super helpful when I need house stuff done. He'll come over and help me light the pilot on my gas fireplace, or troubleshoot when my heater or AC starts giving me trouble."

"Sounds like you've got some really great neighbors," I said.

She nodded. "There are also some younger thirtysomething couples down the street. I don't know those families as well, but it's nice to chat with them and see their little kids. Every year we do a neighborhood Easter egg hunt and a big Halloween costume parade."

"Your neighborhood sounds pretty amazing," I said, and she agreed.

"The thing is," I said, "when you move, even if it's only a few miles, your neighborhood does change. Yes, you can still drive to your book club, no question. But you can't be quite so carefree about drinking wine when you have to get into a car instead of just strolling back across the street. And your neighborhood—there's something to it. There's something about chatting over the fence or running into a neighbor at the grocery store."

I reminded Tessa that if she were to move farther than a mile or two—say 15 miles—then it's a big deal. Moving is always a big deal, but at that distance, you're definitely relocating your life to some extent. She would probably stop going to the book club eventually, even if at the beginning she tried to keep it up. If she moved to a new county or a new city, she might also need to find a new dentist, doctors, and other healthcare providers, as well as establishing other commercial and professional relationships. That includes the places she frequents on a day-to-day basis: grocery stores, dry cleaners, cafés and restaurants, hair and nail salons.

If you live in Atlanta and move to Alpharetta? That may be only a 30- to 40-minute drive, but in some ways, you might as well have moved out of state. Sure, you can still see people. You can always make the drive. But proximity is important. As we've discussed, it's already more of a challenge to keep up your social network during retirement; once you throw physical distance into the mix, it's an even bigger obstacle.

When your geography changes, so does your community. The intangibles—seeing kids, grandkids, friends—change dramatically with a long-distance move. Though I should note that if your adult children live 40 minutes (or miles) away, that still checks the HROB box for living close to at least half of your kids.

"Are you close to your friends and family?" I asked Tessa.

"Yes! My daughter lives about 10 minutes away. And most of my friends live nearby."

I gently reminded her that if she moved to another county, she would most likely lose touch with some of her current friends and have to make new ones. But I said I also understood why the thought of keeping her old routines was painful, now that her husband was gone. After all, most of her friends had been their couple friends, and no one else had lost a spouse. That didn't stop Tessa's friends from being empathetic and loving—they brought her flowers, cooked casseroles, and sat with her while she cried. But it was still hard.

As for the house itself? Tessa was deeply conflicted. She loved the house, but she felt like there were reminders of her husband everywhere. She hadn't been able to empty out his office; even looking at his lonely pillow made her sad. And there was clutter everywhere. She was the first to admit she hadn't done a very good job keeping things tidy amid her grief.

"Some of our neighbors recently sold their house," Tessa told me, "and they said it's a very good seller's market for homes in our area. If I want to get top dollar, doesn't that mean I should act now?"

I explained to Tessa how, if the houses in her neighborhood were selling for top dollar, so were the houses in most other neighborhoods. She might be able to get top dollar, but she'd also be paying top dollar for another house anywhere in the same vicinity. If she wanted to sell her place for $550,000, which was the number she had in mind, a similar house that she liked and felt comfortable in was going to cost her at least the same amount somewhere else. If she moved farther away, we'd land right back at the 30-to-40-minutes-away conversation. The only way for her to make a sell-then-buy move financially attractive was to relocate somewhere that, at least geographically speaking, was dramatically different. And at that point, you might as well move out of state because you're going to have to reestablish not just your neighborhood but your entire social network.

I said all this to Tessa, but it didn't dissuade her. While she wasn't sure if she was truly emotionally ready to move, she told me she had taken steps to list her home for sale.

"It's a bittersweet decision," she told me. "I still feel conflicted about it. But I have to see where this leads."

So Tessa put the house on the market. She hired a professional stager, who told her she needed to do a good bit of work before her home would sell. The whole place needed to be decluttered and deep cleaned. The basement, which Tessa and her husband had primarily used for storage, was in dire need of a glow-up, a coat of fresh paint on the walls and concrete floors.

"We need new art," the stager said, "better furniture and some bright new rugs. And you'll want to hire someone to wash all the windows to really make them gleam. If you want to get top dollar for this house—and this is a pretty hot market in Atlanta—you're going to need to spend a little time and money to spruce this place up."

Tessa said, "OK. Let's do it."

So she scheduled the window washers. She called a handyman and a 1-800-GOT-JUNK-type service to come clean out the basement. While they were there, she realized she had junk all over the place, not just the basement. Tessa cleared out the master bedroom and the family den. She even recruited a couple of her book club friends to help her clean out her husband's office. These women were happy to help.

"If we're going to do this right," Tessa said, "then let's really tidy this place up."

By the end of the week, the windows had been washed and the whole house had been decluttered. Tessa bought new rugs and a few pieces of not-too-expensive furniture from Pottery Barn and some gorgeous wall art at Pier 1. She got a new kitchen tablecloth, cream pillows and sheets for the master bedroom, and a lavender comforter set for the guest room. She changed all the light bulbs, dusted the fixtures, polished the sconces—a lot of little stuff that added up.

The stager suggested putting in a bigger flatscreen TV in the main living room. At first Tessa demurred—until she went online and saw how inexpensive it would be. She discarded her old clunker television from 1999 and got a TV big enough for all her kids and grandkids to crowd around for Disney movie nights.

Tessa's house didn't just look better. It looked spectacular. It looked like a new house! Not only did it sparkle—it smiled. All she had to do was roll up her sleeves and put a little work into it. As it turned out, staying active also helped Tessa move through her grief. She said she felt like she was finally coming back to life.

Can you see where this is going?

Tessa dressed up her house to sell it, only to realize: "Wait a minute. I don't want to go!" Not only did she have a refreshed house that she remembered she loved; it looked better than ever. And she didn't have to say goodbye to her neighbors and friends. There was no reason for her to leave.

Tidy-Up Tessa is still there to this day. If you ask her, she'll tell you how happy she is that she didn't pull the trigger on the sale of her house, but rather stayed in her beloved home.

When it comes to houses, the grass is always a little bit greener on the other side. That's especially true when your neighbor keeps a well-manicured lawn. Very few of us love every single thing about our home. There's always something we want to change or update.

Houses are not forever organisms. They leak, crack, fall into disrepair. They require a lot of maintenance as they slowly disintegrate over time. Most of us have at one time or another thought: "Hey, it'd be nice to have a new house. A fresh start." I totally get that sentiment.

But *the happiest retirees know that neighborhoods and networks are more important than their four walls.* Sometimes, when you're exhausting yourself looking everywhere for the perfect place to fix all your problems, you might realize yours was the best nest all along.[3]

That said, there's no statistic that says that if you move, you'll be unhappy. We've met plenty of extremely happy retirees in this book who have moved. Mary McCormick went to Big Canoe, and Paradise Paula went to the Florida Panhandle—both secondary homes that became their primary ones. Frank and Ava Johnson moved to California to be closer to their kids.

I'm not saying there's one course of action that's right for every retiree. What I *am* saying is that HROBs recognize the immense value of their neighborhoods and networks. Mary, Paula, Frank, and Ava all made a conscious choice to move *toward* family, core pursuits, and social connections, not away from them.

DON'T BE A DEBBIE DOWNER

We're all familiar with the story of Don and Debbie Downer, even if we know them by other names. Now that Don and Debbie are retired and their kids are grown with kids of their own, the Downers don't need a two-story, four-bedroom house in the heart of Atlanta, right? They've decided to downsize.

Bad news, Don and Debbie: the moving truck might be dropping you off on the *unhappy* block of your new neighborhood.

Happy retirees don't downsize. My research has shown that the people who said they didn't plan to downsize were more likely to be happy, and those who planned to downsize were more likely to be unhappy.

How do I interpret that data? In a couple of ways. If you need to sell your home, maybe you haven't been able to pay off the mortgage, so you never freed yourself from that financial and mental burden. Perhaps you don't love your neighborhood all that much to begin with. Unlike Tidy-Up Tessa, maybe you don't get along with your neighbors, and there are no Easter egg hunts and happy hours masquerading as book clubs.

Personally, I think it goes deeper. I believe the real reason happy retirees *don't* downsize is emotional. They love their neighborhoods, and they've established themselves in their communities. They feel genuine safety, trust, and intimacy within their social networks. That tracks, considering HROBs feel connected to the people around them, "plugged in" in all the ways that count.

Best of all, they like having a place where friends and family can gather. They know their kids and grandkids are going to come home to visit, and they want space to host everyone. Their homes become the warm, cozy nexus for birthdays and holidays—Mother's Day brunches, Fourth of July BBQ cookouts, Thanksgiving dinners. And don't forget the bridal showers and baby showers, all the various celebrations that mark the most wonderful parts of a life.

The happiest retirees understand that a home is so much more than a mortgage. It's more than a foundation, roof, and four walls. Home is where the heart is, a place where the people you love can come together around a crackling fire, sit side-by-side at a long harvest table, and feast on joy, health, and happiness until the cows come home.

Investing Habits

BE A TOMORROW INVESTOR

In the Paleolithic era, two of our ancestors walked through the Kalahari Desert. The men spoke of life in the village—which hunters had brought home the biggest, meatiest kills, which basket weavers created the most beautiful baskets. As they walked side by side, they heard a slight rustle in the bush.

The first man wasted no time. He sprinted away immediately, fleeing to the safety of the village and into the arms of his own lovely basket weaver, the woman who sat by the fire awaiting his return.

The second guy thought, "There's really a 99 percent probability that it's just wind blowing through the—"

He didn't finish. A bristle-maned lion leapt out of the bush and ate him.

We are the descendants of the first man, the one who immediately escaped and lived to tell the tale. We have been genetically programmed for thousands of years to evade danger, to avoid risk. None other than Harvard Medical School confirmed "the fight-or-flight response evolved as a survival mechanism, enabling people and other mammals to react quickly to life-threatening situations."[1] Fight or flight is in our DNA.

Unfortunately, this wiring typically runs counter to being a good investor.

Though today's world presents many challenges, I think it's safe to say death by lion isn't common. But as my wife would be the first to tell you: men's brains are slow to evolve. Our biological fight-or-flight response is often triggered by non-life-threatening events. Once our hackles are up, it's difficult to make calm, objective decisions.

Take Panic Paul, the 64-year-old CEO of a shipping company. One sunny morning, Paul gets a phone call from Anxiety Andrew about a great stock tip for Company A. "You've got to get in while it's hot," says Andrew, "or you're going to miss your chance."

A separate call from Emotional Emory really sends Paul over the edge. Emory and Paul both own stock in Company B, a tech startup that isn't doing well due to a microchip shortage.

"I remember 2008," Emory says with a shudder, "and I don't ever want to live through that again. I'm going to sell before things get really bad. You should, too."

Panic Paul is not a sophisticated investor. He enjoys it as a hobby, but he's prone to moving money around on a whim, even when his financial advisor begs him not to. He's not the most measured of investors. His name is Panic Paul, after all.

So he completely overwrites his portfolio. Despite the protests of his advisor, he sells his stock in Company B, puts a portion of the proceeds in Company A, and leaves the rest in cash.

Bad idea. Panic Paul let his fight-or-flight response control his investing habits. He allowed his reptilian brain to overtake his human one. Paul escaped the imaginary danger of the bristle-maned lion, only to run straight into the very real danger of bad investing.

There are entire books on this topic. Investor behavior—the emotion that comes with being an investor—is perhaps the largest variable and determinant of investor success. Investing is an inherently emotional process that encompasses the full range of feelings from greed and euphoria to fear and avoidance.

But it is possible—and vitally important—to control our fear, lest we make impulsive or irrational decisions.[2] When it comes to investing, I am asking you to stare into the face of thousands of years of conditioning and genetic wiring and say, "There is another way." Plenty of people have come before you and chosen a path of wisdom instead of fear, prudence instead of panic. And they have lived to tell the tale.

There are several core investment habits that clearly separate the happiest retirees from the unhappiest. In this chapter, I'll share a number of inalienable truths, including:

- **Stock dividend income trumps bond income by an incredibly large margin.** Dividend investing is one of the most powerful tools in the HROB's toolkit—as long as you use it the right way.

- **Investment success is less about perfection and more about participation.** If you're trying to chase the fluctuations of the market, focused on buying stock at the "perfect" time, you're setting yourself up for failure. If you have time, you've got time.

- **Losing money feels twice as bad as making money feels good.** This is one of those strange equations that doesn't make logical sense but is absolutely true. Unhappy retirees want to feel good in the moment, so they're reactive. Happy retirees know to take the long view.

- **Happy retirees do not make investment decisions based on emotion.** They are not fueled by fear. They take time to take stock. (Pun totally intended.)

- **HROBs are tomorrow investors, not today investors.**
  Contrary to what you may think, volatility is actually your friend. The happiest retirees know how to find a strategy and stick to that strategy.

Don't worry. I won't let that lion get you. With a little acuity, smart investing, and fine-tuned patience, *you'll* be the one bringing the biggest kill home.

THE POWER OF DIVIDEND INVESTING: THE APPLE OF YOUR EYE

Hear ye, hear ye! Are you ready for a proclamation? I proudly and loudly proclaim my staunch belief in dividend investing. Take a look at Figure 11.1.

If there was ever a chart to remember as an investor, it's this one. It doesn't chronicle one magical stock purchase that climbed to the moon. Instead, it tells the story of an unassuming force that creates a rising source of income for a lifetime. It's the story of stock dividends, which have proven to grow at twice the rate of inflation over the better part of stock market history. In fact, though it's commonly believed that bonds are the conservative counterpart to stocks, this study compares how an investment in equities for dividend income has fared relative to investing in bonds. The results may surprise you.

Let's compare a $10,000 investment in the S&P 500 vs. the Lehman/Barclays Aggregate Bond Index beginning in 1980. In each case, the investor left the principal alone, while taking the income produced each year to spend. As you can see, income from stock dividends is shown in white, and income from bonds (interest) is shown filled in.

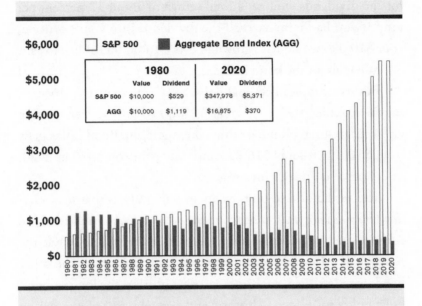

	1980		2020	
	Value	Dividend	Value	Dividend
S&P 500	$10,000	$529	$347,978	$5,371
AGG	$10,000	$1,119	$16,875	$370

FIGURE 11.1 **Stock Dividends vs. Bond Interest**
Source: Capital Investment Advisors

In the very first year, a $10,000 investment in the S&P 500 paid a dividend of about $529, or 5.29 percent on the initial investment. At the end of 2020, after 41 years, the dividend income shown by the white line climbed to about $5,371. That's a 53 percent annual yield on the original investment.

This shows that the income from stock dividends grew at about 6 percent per year. Inflation during that same period grew at about 3 percent. That means dividends increased at *double* the rate of inflation. Talk about protecting your purchasing power!

But don't forget that the investment corpus grew as well. In addition to the income you received each year, your $10,000 investment would have grown into more than $347,000.

This price-only return (which excludes dividend income) clocks in at about 9 percent per year. If you add in another 3 percent for the dividends, you get a total return of about 12 percent per year. If you had reinvested all the dividends into your portfolio, your $10,000 would have grown to over $1,000,000 after 41 years.

What about the bond interest?

Bonds are typically thought of as a safer alternative to stocks—maybe *too* safe. They were great in 1980 when you were getting an 11 interest rate. But over time, the Aggregate Bond Index grew from $10,000 to only $16,875 and only paid you $370 in 2020, or 2.2 percent on your investment.

The verdict, based on the data in our study, is that *stock dividend income wins against bond income by an incredibly large margin.* Annual stock dividend income increased over 10-fold, while the remaining price-only return grew 35-fold. Bonds, on the other hand, rose less than two times in price (during the longest bond bull market we've seen in history) and experienced a 67 percent reduction in income.

It doesn't matter if you have $500,000, $5 million, or $50 million in your retirement portfolio. It's hard to find a more consistent source of growing income to outpace inflation, along with the potential for a dramatic increase in your underlying principal: 35 times the value of your investment, and 10 times your annual income.[3]

When you look at these historical studies, you might say to yourself, "That would have been nice over the last 40 years, Wes, but haven't I missed the boat?"

Not really. If you're 40 or 50 years old, don't you have three to four decades left to invest? Don't listen to that fearful voice whispering, "It's too late." Remember that you have more years of spending ahead of you than you might think. Think Galapagos tortoise life expectancy here: decades, not years.

Now, imagine looking specifically for stocks that are perennial dividend payers and consistent dividend growers. Searching and finding these investments can be a worthy lifetime pursuit for any investor with long-term patience and vision.

In my personal experience as both an investor and an investment strategist, dividend investing helps me keep my emotions in check. The swells of the stock market are big and choppy. If you panic with every rise and fall, you'll never make it back to shore. Better to keep your eyes on the horizon.

In contrast to price moves, stock dividend income is typically very steady. There are dozens and dozens of companies that have paid consistent and rising dividends for 10, 20, 30, even 50 years or more. This means cash flow is recurring and something that people can actually live on.

Dividend investing is like an apple tree. I know apple orchards well: when I was 16, I worked at an orchard in West Chester, Pennsylvania. It was wonderful. When done correctly, dividend investing allows you to live off the apples without having to chop off any big, beautiful branches. You don't want to destroy the tree by over-consumption—you want your kids and grandkids to be able to hang a rope swing from its giant boughs. If you let it continue to mature and grow, it can keep bearing fruit for years to come.

As long as you nurture your tree with sunlight and water, it will continue to yield apples and give you plenty of pleasant shade during your golden years. Furthermore, whereas a 10-year-old apple tree might grow 200 apples in a season, a 15-year-old one might grow 300. A bigger tree means more apples. Likewise, a bigger investment portfolio means more income potential. How do you make it grow? The answer is the same for apples or investments: time and care.

I have fond memories of my time among the apple trees, and I want you to feel the same fondness for the fruits of your portfolio. Take this advice and bake it into a delicious happy-retirement pie.

PURCHASING POWER

Investing is often thought of as a means of growing your over-all nest egg, liquid assets, portfolio value, and net worth. But really, the whole purpose of investing is to protect your purchasing power, aka spending power. Meaning, if you lived on $75,000 per year while you were working, you want to continue to live on that equivalent, for the next 20 to 30 years.

Here's the catch. You have to account for inflation. So it's not actually $75,000—it's $75,000 *plus inflation*, which is ultimately $100,000 or $150,000 over time. So, yes, you are investing for the nest egg to grow, but the crux of everything is to protect your pur-chasing power. And there are few other assets that enable you to do so like stocks. Bonds can sometimes pay plenty of income, but they aren't usually able to grow income over time.

PERFECT IS THE ENEMY OF THE GOOD: PARTICIPATION VERSUS PERFECTION

A radio listener recently called in to *Money Matters* with a press-ing question.

"The market is near an all-time high, Wes," she said, "and I've been sitting in cash for half of my portfolio. I feel like I missed out and want to get back in at some point. When do I get into stocks? Do I wait until the market drops, then jump in?"

As investors, we often feel like we must have good timing to achieve investment success. It's only natural to wonder if we should have more money in the market. No one wants to have bad timing, whether it's the "unlucky" investor or the guy who makes a bad joke in a wedding toast.

Something I frequently tell the families I work with to reassure them is, if you have time, you've got time. In other words, if you have years, not months, the amount of time you are invested handily trumps how you timed your purchase, or when you "got in."

Of course, we all want to buy low and sell high. But unfortunately, we don't have a Stargate in our bedrooms to clue us in on what markets will do next week or next month. Herein lies the basic conundrum of investing: it's simply impossible to know the future.

"So what if we strategize to wait for a correction?" you say. Even if we do and we get one, it's widely understood that most investors won't actually pull the trigger when markets are down. The very fear that led to the correction is what stops investors from buying in when markets swoon.

The real answer lies in the data. When we look at the difference in growth between getting in the market (using the S&P 500) at the "perfect" time versus getting in the market at the "worst" time. The numbers don't lie. Check out Figure 11.2.

These data points illustrate how an investment of $10,000 in the S&P 500 can grow over a particular period of time. Each period is relevant in that those specific years were on the precipice of a stock market correction. It obviously takes time to recover from any downturn, so the data points show what you would have as of mid-2021 if you had chosen to invest the $10,000 during each unique starting point.

The data gives us the results for "perfect" market timing (meaning when the correction is at its nadir) and the "worst" market timing (meaning right before the market dipped), versus simply holding your money in cash or CDs (risk free).

Here's how the numbers compare for the time periods of a 23- and 21-year long run, 14- and 10-year intermediate runs, and 3- and 1-year short runs.

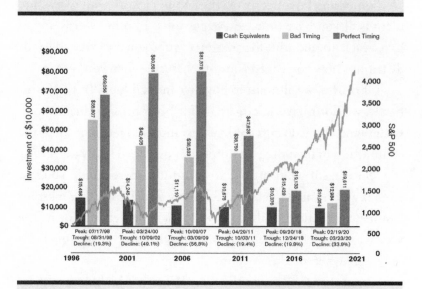

FIGURE 11.2 **Participation Is More Important
Than Perfection When Investing**

Note: Bloomberg L.P. Stocks are represented by the S&P 500,
and cash equivalents by the Bloomberg Barclays U.S. Treasury Bill Index.
Indexes are unmanaged, do not incur fees or expenses, and cannot be
invested directly. This chart represents a hypothetical investment and is for
illustrative purposes only. Dividends and interest are assumed to have
been reinvested, and the example does not reflect the effects of taxes,
expenses, or fees. The actual annual rate of return will fluctuate with
market conditions. Past performance is no guarantee of future results.
Investing involves risk, including potential loss of principal.
Please refer to the disclosures for additional information.
Source: Capital Investment Advisors

- **Long run (23 years), investing in 1998.** In 1998, the
  market saw a near–20 percent correction. Investing at the
  "perfect" time (the bottom of the correction) shows growth
  to $69,000, while investing at the "worst" time (right
  before the correction) shows growth to about $56,000.
  Holding cash/CDs would have resulted in $15,500.

- **Long run (21 years), investing during the 2000–2002 period.** Oh, yes, we all remember the tech crash. It was massive: the S&P 500 went down more than 49 percent. Getting in the market with "perfect" timing yielded growth to $80,500. Getting in with the "worst" timing yielded growth to $42,500. Cash grew to $14,000. Here, investing at the "worst" time still bested cash by nearly 200 percent.

- **Intermediate run (14 years), investing during the 2007–2009 period.** Just like the tech crash, the Great Recession market period is fresh in our memories. During this time, "perfect" timing yielded growth to $81,500. The "worst" timing yielded growth to $36,500. Cash only grew to $11,000, as interest rates were near zero during this span. Investing at the "worst" time still beat cash by 229 percent.

- **Intermediate run (10 years), investing in 2011.** This time period again saw another near–20 percent correction. "Perfect" time investing yielded growth to $47,500. "Worst" time investing yielded growth to $38,750. Again, cash offered very little upside, garnering growth of a modest $675. This time, the "worst" timing beat cash by 263 percent.

- **Short run (3 years), investing in 2018.** Similar to 2011, stocks again corrected a near-20 percent. "Perfect" time investing yielded growth to $19,000. "Worst" time investing yielded growth to $15,500. While cash returned a meager $375. In less than three years, the "worst" timing still beat cash by nearly 50 percent.

- **Short run (1 year), investing in 2020.** Last, but certainly not least, came the Covid-19-induced selloff in March 2020. Although it felt like an eternity at the time, this was by far the quickest selloff on the list as stocks sank 34 percent in just 23 trading days. "Perfect" time investing yielded growth to $19,500. "Worst" time investing yielded growth to $13,000. Cash was virtually flat, returning just $54. In a matter of just over a year, the "worst" timing still beat cash by 29 percent.

Understanding this market history helps us focus on what really matters when it comes to investing. News flash: *investment success is less about perfection and more about participation.* In every scenario outlined, investing at the "worst" time bested holding cash by a long shot.

Because here's the thing. Market drops are very normal and should be *expected,* as indicated by Figure 11.3. Despite the S&P 500 Index being positive in 31 of 41 years, the market's average

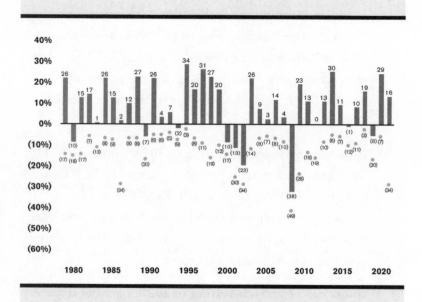

FIGURE 11.3 **Intra-Year Stock Market Declines**
Source: Capital Investment Advisors

intra-year decline is 14.3 percent. This is proof that market corrections (10 percent or more declines) are to be expected, as an "average" decline in any given year is almost 15 percent.

This market history reminds us again of the importance of time. And when I say time, I don't mean 100 years. We're talking 5, 8, 15 years. Every one of you reading this has that much time. At least we hope that's the case. You're eating well, right? If not, just wait for the *You Can Cook Better Than You Think* cookbook . . .

Hopefully, this answers the question that's been nagging at you. Don't beat yourself up for failing to "get in" at the perfect time. That's not the right approach anyway. While we tend to think about investing in terms of what our money may be worth in a year or two, that's the wrong math. Make time and participation your North Star as you set sail, not the unrealistic goal of market timing perfection.

Grab your high-powered telescope and look out over the next five years at least. And 10 years? Land ahoy!

Bond. James Bond. Or My Grudging Thoughts on Conservative Assets

Just about every three or four years, the market drops 20 percent on average. With that in mind, it can be a good idea to own a certain percentage of your overall portfolio in conservative assets such as bonds. If you translate those numbers into years, it gives you some psychological peace of mind and provides an opportunity to extend the time horizon of your riskier investments.

Despite my frequent lack of enthusiasm for bonds, I think one of their greatest powers is the Zen tranquility they can bring.

Do they pay as much as stocks? Usually no. Do they appreciate as much as stocks? Usually no. Then why do we own them?

Easy: because they do win in the peace-of-mind category.

Investors tend to think in terms of percentages. "This percentage of my portfolio is in stocks, while this percentage is in bonds, etc." Happy retirees can look at the amount of their conservative assets and translate that into spending money over years and months, which gives them a long time horizon on the riskier, more volatile assets. Time is our best friend, perhaps even our most important ally, when it comes to investing and letting stocks grow. So I give a begrudging kiss to the boring but stable bond market.

Consider your portfolio stirred, not shaken.

KEEP CALM AND CARRY ON

Remember our friend Panic Paul? It probably won't surprise you that he is not an HROB. Unhappy retirees exhibit a heightened sense of emotion around their investment portfolios. Like Paul, they frequently confuse clickbait headlines, news stories, and market volatility for a permanent threat, when really these are temporary upsets.

Here's a fascinating peek into the human psyche: *losing money feels twice as bad as making money feels good.* This is called "loss aversion," and it's a cornerstone of the Prospect Theory, which landed Daniel Kahneman a Nobel Prize in Economics.[4] Kahneman posits that humans are more keenly aware of losses than gains. In a Yale study, a researcher would offer a monkey two pieces of apple for a token, but sometimes only give one. Another researcher would offer the monkey one piece of apple, but sometimes surprise them with another. Despite averaging out to the same amount of apple pieces, the monkeys favored the "bonus" researcher.

We see this play out in investing time and time again. I learned early on in this industry that an account that went from $1 million to $1.5 million, and then down to $1.3 million, was viewed as a loss of $200,000 instead of a gain of $300,000.

In sports terms, if a team is up big at halftime and ends up barely winning, people criticize its performance. No one says, "Congrats on scoring enough points in the first half to slightly outweigh your poor performance in the second!" Once a portfolio reaches $1.5 million, it is always expected to be at or above $1.5 million. Irrational much?

If you want to be a happy retiree, stick to reason and good sense. *HROBs do not make investment decisions based on emotion.* They refuse to let their fight-or-flight reflexes take over rational thought, steering them offtrack as investors. Your best bet is to be stoically invested over a long period of time, no matter what happens. Volatility gets a bad rap, but it is actually our friend.[5]

Happy retirees are tomorrow investors, not today investors. That's a term I coined for my smart, savvy clients who know it doesn't serve them to have a myopic view of the market. They understand that they are investing in an economy that will grow over time. As long as we have a basket of solid companies, the market (and our portfolio) is likely to continue to expand and grow along with the US economy.

You have to remember that, unless you're a trader—and if you're reading this book, I'm going to assume you're not—you are investing for tomorrow. Yes, the waters may be choppy. No one said this journey wouldn't make you seasick. But HROBs are the ones standing calmly on the sturdy ship they've built, steady amid the giant swells, as they exclaim, "Hark! What do I see on the horizon? 'Tis dry land!"

Even as we are bombarded with the sensationalized headlines of today, we need only fix our eyes on the smooth shores of tomorrow. Or as the Brits would tell us: keep calm and carry on.

How do we do that? By choosing a strategy and then staying the course. You can absolutely execute this on your own, but this is often where retirees need the player-coach, aka advisor. And this isn't a plug. If you need help to get to your goal, then by all means, find an investment advisor—any investment advisor—who is both informed and objective.

Statistics show that around 30 percent of investors feel good about going it alone, while 70 percent say, "Hey, I need some help with this." Not just to manage the money in an appropriate way but to manage it toward a particular goal: having X amount of money in retirement every month, or X number of dollars at age 75, or being able to own a second home so the kids can come visit at the beach.

HROBs have a definitive strategy that works for them. There are thousands to choose from, almost countless ways to manage your money. It's not so important to pick the perfect way, but to pick *a* way—and then stick to it.

TODAY, TOMORROW, TO AMERICA

Let's recap what we know about happy retirees from an investment standpoint. First of all, they understand that their goal is to protect their purchasing power. Yes, they are focused on growing their portfolio, but their primary goal is to have the portfolio provide a steady amount of income that keeps up with or outpaces inflation.

In order to do that, HROBs focuses on what they have control over. Their income comes from stock dividends, and they eat the apples from that tree rather than cutting off its branches.

Unhappy retirees cannot tune out the financial gurus and talking heads or put distance between themselves and the scary news du jour. They are glued to their television and computer screens, unable to look away from the declines that happen in markets on any given day, week, month, or year. Look away!

What's true in life is true in investing: nothing is going to be perfect all the time. Perfection isn't possible anyway. HROBs understand that participation is more important than perfection. They know emotions can kill your investments. They are proud tomorrow investors, not reactive investors of today.

So what does tomorrow look like for us in America? My opinion is that there are three possible answers:

1. Tomorrow is good.

2. Tomorrow is great.

3. Tomorrow is all of the above.

I truly believe that.

The happiest retirees know that when times are tough or the political climate goes sideways, America will stay strong. Just because the political party of your choice doesn't win an election cycle doesn't mean the rest of the economy is going to hit a wall, even if it may appear to do so temporarily.

If you want to invest, you must place your trust in this great country. The economy itself is an army of American productivity, and it will continue to march forward over time. The happiest retirees know this. It gives them hope and conviction for the future—for themselves, for their children, for their grandchildren, and for many generations to come.

CHAPTER 12

Spending Habits

UNDERSTANDING THE POWER OF
THE 4 PERCENT *PLUS* RULE

One recent spring morning, I had the great honor of interviewing David Bach for my radio show. David is a legend, a financial expert, coach, and all-around great guy. He has multiple *New York Times* bestsellers, including *The Automatic Millionaire*, *Smart Women Finish Rich*, and his latest title, *The Latte Factor*, with more than 7 million books in print. He's been translated into more than 20 languages. If you write about money, David Bach is who you aspire to be. I'm lucky to call him a friend.

Back in 2018, I interviewed David in New York City about *The Latte Factor*. If you go to the official website, you'll see the book is based on "the simple idea that all you need to do to finish rich is to look at the small things you spend your money on every day and see whether you could redirect that spending to yourself. Putting aside as little as a few dollars a day for your future rather than spending it on little purchases such as lattes, bottled water, fast food, cigarettes, magazines and so on, can really make a difference between accumulating wealth and living paycheck to paycheck."[1]

The origin story of the Latte Factor is fascinating. It came from a retirement seminar David did some 20-odd years ago during which a young woman raised her hand and said, "I don't have enough to put in my 401(k)."

Sitting on the desk beside her was a Starbucks coffee cup and one of those waxy brown bags holding a scone.

David nodded toward the coffee and scone.

"What did those cost you?" he asked.

"I don't know the exact amount," she said. "Five or six bucks?"

"If you spend five or sick bucks on a coffee and scone every day," David said, "it starts to add up to real money."

Then he did what all great financial gurus do: whipped out his nifty compounding calculator.

Let's do the math right now, adjusted for 2021 prices. A skinny vanilla latte at Starbucks will set you back about five bucks. A blueberry scone is around three. We'll call it an even $8. That means you're spending an average of $240 a month, or $2,880 a year.

Now let's say that, instead of buying a latte and scone, you invest that money.

We'll assume an estimated interest rate of 10 percent over a 35-year time span which is less than the 11 percent the S&P 500 has averaged over the last 35 years. If the young woman was 25 when she took David's seminar, that means she'd be 60 by the time she takes the money out. We'll select a daily compound frequency, meaning the times per year that interest will be compounded.

If you had a compound calculator like David, and you put in all those numbers, it would look a little something like Figure 12.1.

Ready for the magic?

Figure 12.2 shows how much she'd have in 35 years.

The results are in! And no, you didn't read that wrong.

Her $8 a day has grown to $924,732.74.[2]

Almost one million dollars.

Step 1: Initial Investment	
Initial Investment Amount of money that you have available to invest initially.	$8.00
Step 2: Contribute	
Monthly Contribution Amount that you plan to add to the principal every month, or a negative number for the amount that you plan to withdraw every month.	$240.00
Length of Time in Years Length of time, in years, that you plan to save.	35
Step 3: Interest Rate	
Estimated Interest Rate Your estimated annual interest rate.	10
Interest Rate Variance Range Range of interest rates (above and below the rate set above) that you desire to see results for.	0
Step 4: Compound It	
Compound Frequency Times per year that interest will be compounded.	Daily

Calculate   Reset

FIGURE 12.1 **Cost of a Latte, Part I**

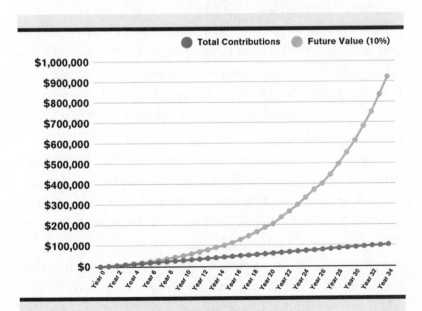

FIGURE 12.2 **Cost of a Latte, Part II**

With a number like that, who needs caffeine?

The irony of the Latte Factor, of course, is that it's not really about lattes. The latte is just a metaphor for wasteful spending, and wasteful spending adds up. In this way, David and I share a common belief about money: *spend only on what brings you joy*.

The other great irony is that, when I chatted with David at a quaint New York bar back in 2018, he told me he was thinking about heading to Italy, the coffee capital of the world. (Fun fact: *latte* is the Italian word for milk. Next time you order a skinny latte, just keep in mind that you actually just ordered a skinny milk.)

I figured David was going for an extended trip, maybe two or three weeks. A month later, I saw him posting pics on Instagram. He was still in Italy.

More months passed. He was still there, living *la bella vita*.

Finally, I sent him a note. "You still in Italy, David?"

"Yep," he wrote back. "We'll be here for at least a year."

I was blown away. David had packed up his family and business in New York City—and moved to the cradle of the Renaissance with his wife and two young teenagers. Nearly two years later, the Bachs are still there, living a few blocks from Ponte Vecchio, the iconic bridge in the heart of Florence. They're having the time of their lives.

During our most recent conversation for the Retire Sooner podcast, David took the call from his Italian villa, for which he pays less in rent than he paid for just the HOA and property tax on his condo in New York. He told me a story I hadn't heard before, one that will stay with me forever. A couple of years ago, after he spoke at a retirement seminar, a couple in their early sixties approached him. They didn't look very healthy. In fact, they weren't. They told him they both had cancer: she was stage III; he was stage IV.

"David," the man said, "I suspect a guy like you has the money thing figured out. Can I give you some advice? Don't wait to travel. Don't wait until you're our age and lose your health. You're in your fifties. You can work from anywhere. You should travel *now*, while you still can."

There he was, David Bach, the man who gave advice, now receiving it. So what did he do?

He made a plan, got his finances in order, and moved to Italy. I bet he even enjoys a cappuccino now and then. He's earned it.

In this chapter, we will:

- **Unlock the power of the 4 Percent *Plus* Rule.** This is the easiest and simplest way to know how much you can safely spend during retirement—and it's the guiding principle for HROBs. If you think you know this one, think again: it's gotten a major modern face-lift since its origins in the early 1990s.

- **Discover the happiest retirees are smart spenders— they're "masters of the middle."** They don't spend lavishly, but they're not parsimonious misers, either. They know how to both save and spend with balance and an eye to the future.

- **Reexamine the Rich Ratio, the simplest way to measure how much money you have, related to how much you need.** This simple formula can alter the way you look at your current financial situation—and utterly transform the way you improve it.

- **Understand it's never too late to save for retirement.** You can start to save at any age and still become the Happiest Retiree on the Block.

THE 4 PERCENT *PLUS* RULE: THE ARTIST FORMERLY KNOWN AS 4 PERCENT

We're going to rewind the clock, hurtling back through space and time until we arrive at a kinder, simpler era.

The year is 2014. *You Can Retire Sooner Than You Think* has just hit the shelves. In it, I talk about the 4 Percent Rule. Maybe you remember.

The 4 Percent Rule is a piece of financial planning wisdom from venerable financial planner William Bengen, who made waves with this bold declaration in 1994. The rule is meant to help you determine what percent of your retirement portfolio you can withdraw yearly, adjusted for inflation, to ensure you will never have to worry about running out of money.

It's a little equation with a *lot* of horsepower. You *take your starting retirement balance, multiply by 4 percent, and adjust that amount up for inflation*, year after year—provided you have the right asset mix of between 50 and 70 percent perennially in stocks.

Let's say you have $1 million in your retirement portfolio. $1 million × 4% = $40,000 in year one. If inflation is 5 percent, your new withdrawal level ratchets up to $42,000 the next year, and so on.

The 4 Percent Rule is a time-tested guideline that helps us figure out the *maximum* amount you can pull from your savings and still have money left. Because that's what retirees want to know. "What's the *most* I can take and still make my money last a really long time?" It's helpful to have a rule we can work with, and this is a solid one. The 4 Percent Rule has been a staple of financial planning for as long as I've been in the industry.

That is, until 2021.

It's not often I get multiple text messages about the same article in *Barron's*, particularly when it's about a specific rule or strategy.

In the world of financial planning, very rarely is there ever breaking news. It's more like watching a glacier melt.

But in January 2021, I woke up to breaking news gone viral—at least "viral" in the financial planning community. Ready for the most incendiary headline you've ever read?

> **The Originator of the 4 Percent Rule, William Bengen,**
> **Thinks It's Off the Mark.**
> **He Says It Now Could Be Up to 4.5 Percent.**[3]

Hold on to your hats, ladies and gents. A financial planning rule of thumb had changed . . . drumroll, please . . . by one-half of 1 percent.

I jest, but this is actually a big deal. Though the headline might not be "Tar Heels Win NCAA Basketball Championship," it's huge if you're trying to afford retirement every month or are planning what year you can retire. At face value, 4 to 4.5 percent might not sound like much—until you realize that hike is basically a 12.5 percent raise (Figure 12.3).

This small but important shift could accelerate your retirement date by months, even years. It's like hyperfuel for the Retire Sooner podcast and my dream of helping a million Americans retire at least one year sooner. This is the sort of thing that makes me want to dance with happiness.

I'm massively interested in this topic. So much so that only a few years ago, my team and I re-created and updated the 4 Percent Rule. The reason I reworked the original was that I'd read a contrary article in the *Wall Street Journal* (always with the contrary articles) comparing the 4 percent rule to the findings of other statisticians, and questioning whether it was still the right number.[4] In May 2020, Wade Pfau, a professor at the American College of Financial Services in Bryn Mawr, wrote a piece for *Forbes* in which

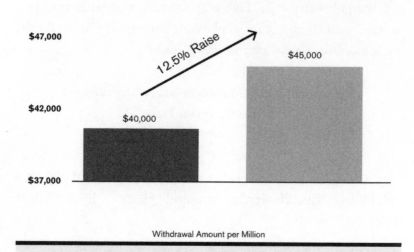

FIGURE 12.3 **Increasing Withdrawal Rate from
4 Percent to 4.5 Percent**

he claimed 4 percent was too high. Pfau believes the new safe withdrawal rate should be at most 3 percent, maybe even as low as 2.4.[5]

Now Bengen is going in the opposite direction, saying that
he's upping the 4 Percent Rule to 4.5. What gives?

As we always do when something exciting happens in the
world of financial planning, my team and I rushed to our calcula-
tors to double-check Bengen's arithmetic.

I come bearing good news. Bengen is no slouch—he has continued to run various iterations of this rule over the last three
decades.

In the original scenario, Bengen recommended that you invest
between 50 and 70 percent of your portfolio in large-cap stocks,
rebalanced annually, and the remaining in bonds. With a 4 percent
withdrawal rate, Figure 12.4 shows how the numbers look.

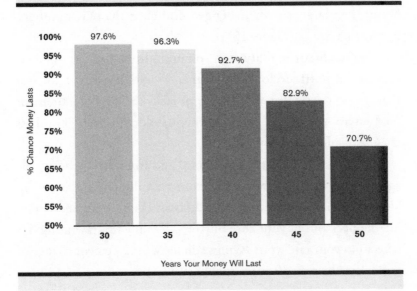

FIGURE 12.4 **The 4 Percent Rule, No Small Caps**

Not bad, right? These numbers are really pretty incredible: 82.9 percent of the time, your money will last 45 years; 92.7 percent of the time, the money lasts 40 years. Even at the high end of the projection, 50 years—and let's be candid: unless Dr. Andrew Steele and his turtle-nerds expedite their research, most of us are not going to have a 50-year retirement—there's a 70.7 percent chance your money will go the distance. Once you get into the more realistic retirement lengths? The 30-, 35-year range? You're edging closer and closer to a 100 percent chance your savings will last as long as you do.

Now let's look at the updated figures. In 2021, Bengen did a little ratio juggling. The basic tenets of the 4 Percent Rule have always been to keep at least 50 percent in large cap stocks. But in *Barron's*, Bengen adjusts the numbers by keeping bonds where they are and redistributing stocks to have 40 percent in large companies and 10 percent in small. Small caps have historically grown a little better than large, so when Bengen crunched the new numbers, here's what he got (Figure 12.5).

You might argue that when you jump from 4 to 4.5, the percentages of portfolio longevity dip at 45 and 50 years. Sure, but that's pie in the sky anyway. That's not really the kind of retirement pie I envision, lying in bed at 106 years old while my grandkids change my diaper.

But let's say you retire early at 60 and live until the feisty ole age of 90, traveling around the country, volunteering at a soup kitchen, spending time with your kids and grandkids, and enjoying the heck out of your core pursuits. If you withdraw using 4.5 percent as your rate, your savings still has a 90.2 percent chance of lasting for the next 30 years. Unbelievable.

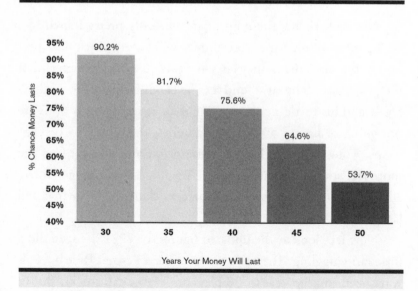

FIGURE 12.5 **The New and Improved 4.5 Percent Rule, with Small Caps**

It won't surprise you that I like these numbers. As I said, that bump from 4 to 4.5 is a 12.5 percent raise in retirement. That money could mean taking one more unforgettable vacation every summer, or investing in a sunny beachside cottage, or simply getting to retire a whole year early and becoming yet another dazzling HROB success story.

I've said it before and I'll say it again: none of this is set in stone. Bengen, Pfau, *WSJ*: they all want to say their piece. I'm less interested in theory and more interested in what these numbers look like in the real world. I want to help retirees pull out the maximum amount from their savings with confidence that they won't outlive their money. And in the real world, somewhere in the 4 to 5 percent range really does work most of the time.

Here's the beauty of this rule: it's dynamic. A dynamic number can go up or down, depending on the specific situation. Consider this me officially putting my stamp on the 4 Percent *Plus* Rule. That's the new gold standard in my book, the rule I use to help thousands of retirees know how much they can spend to stay happy, healthy, and secure.

So hats off to Bengen. It's been a bangin' good time.

Stretching 4 Percent into 5:
The 1,000-Bucks-a-Month Rule

Call me a soothsayer, but years before Bengen shocked the world in 2021, I actually "zhuzhed up" the 4 Percent Rule myself in *You Can Retire Sooner Than You Think*.

By using the 1,000-Bucks-a-Month Rule, which we talked about in Chapter 3, you can actually stretch that 4 percent into 5. The higher withdrawal rate is predicated on two key factors:

income investing and a 5 percent rate without increasing your spending with inflation. Now, not increasing your spending for inflation doesn't sound like the perfect scenario, but if your mortgage is paid off and inflation happens to stay in check for a period of time, this might not be too unrealistic.

Keep in mind that none of these rules are guaranteed. Even the 1,000-Bucks-a-Month Rule is more a "rule of thumb." They're just really good guidelines. If you have a portfolio yield of 4 percent (dividends and interest only) and the portfolio experiences even a little bit of growth/appreciation, *then a 4 percent yield plus 1, 2, or 3 percent in growth over time suggests that you can take out 5 percent almost indefinitely.*

I'm not saying I'm a financial prophet. I'm just looking at the math.

MASTERS OF THE MIDDLE: THE HAPPIEST RETIREES ARE SMART SPENDERS

Meet Howard and Heather Thyme. Howie and Heather retired in their early sixties in the great state of Georgia. Their top core pursuit? Competing in triathlons. The training helps them stay in shape and gives them a way to spend time together, and the races take them to beautiful locations like Hawaii, Western Australia, and Mont Tremblant in Canada. Because the Thymes are HROBs, they look at each of these trips as a wonderful adventure. They want to fully experience the world, not just go home after crossing the finish line.

Triathlons revolve around three of the *ings*—swimming, cycling, and running—all of which you can do at a very reasonable cost. A little amusing, then, that participating in triathlons does not run cheap. You have to pay to enter the official races. Then there are the travel expenses, airfare, hotels, and what you spend when you stick around postrace to enjoy the exotic locales. There are also equipment costs, as you want to make sure you have high-quality bikes. Heather and Howard have been working with a trainer for the last couple of years, so that's an expense, too.

The Thymes came to me and said, "We want to do three different triathlons this year, Wes, and we really want to make the most of them. But we're going to need to take out more than 4 percent of our retirement savings to do it. If we take out a little more than 5 percent, is it the end of the world?"

My answer was no. Why? Because the 4 Percent *Plus* Rule is dynamic.

We ran the numbers and decided they could take out 5.5 percent for two years. That would allow them to do a number of life-changing triathlons. Then, by the time they turned 64, we decided they would start to slow down and do just one triathlon trip each year. Eventually, we were able to find a way to get them under 4 percent to make up for the years they were above it.

Think of it like this. When you set a course for retirement, you've got your withdrawal rate on cruise control. Maybe it's a steady 4 or a smooth 4.5. And it works most of the time. You're cruising along from Georgia all the way down to Florida. But sometimes you've got to put your foot on the brake, so you don't hit a deer on the highway. And every once in a while, you have to hit the accelerator to get you around that nasty 18-wheeler full of swine.

Fast, slow, steady on. None of these speeds are "wrong." The right retirement plan leaves space for all of them, with an understanding that, just as the 4 Percent *Plus* Rule is dynamic, so, too, is the kind of life you want to live.

The Thymes did me proud. They kicked ass and took names at their triathlons, sharing these adventures as a couple and making some of the best memories of their lives. Then, after the glory days as athletic champions, they made the needed adjustments. They reined in their spending to make sure their money would last.

Did it take a little extra planning? Sure. By now, I hope you've figured out that a happy retirement takes time and planning. All the truly good stuff in life does. Marriage. Kids. Training for a triathlon. Tailgating for college football on Saturdays.

But that doesn't mean planning can't be fun. The happiest retirees have a *lot* of fun. They're smart spenders, meaning they're not afraid to spend money on the things that bring them true joy. And they're smart savers, too. Their relationship with spending and saving is fluid. They even splurge now and then, whether it's to take a safari in the Serengeti, put a child through college, or buy a Minnie Winnie, a Winnebago that's "perfectly sized for family adventures" as a way to visit every state in the US of A.[6]

The happiest retirees don't get overextended. While they may have had times in their lives where they had too much in credit card debt or were struggling financially, they always found their way back to center. They have learned how to avoid common financial pitfalls such as mansions, big boats, paying the cost of their children's extended education, or funding their adult children's extravagant lifestyles. You can get in trouble if any of those categories are pushing you beyond your limitations.

HROBs are "masters of the middle." They don't deprive themselves. They can afford to be penny foolish, as long as they're pound wise. If they want to buy a nice Christmas present for their only grandchild, they do it. If they want to eat a nice juicy steak, they order a filet mignon, medium rare.[7]

If they look at their retirement savings and realize they *can* afford to host a big family celebration like Ron and Rita Margarita, they do it.

If they want to take a dream vacation to Africa like Safari Sam, they buy some khakis.

If they want to splurge on a second home tucked into the mountains like (Eat, Drink, and Be) Mary McCormick, they sign on the dotted line.

And if they want a mocha latte, they have invested enough to do so. They drink it with no apology—and no regrets.

THE RICH RATIO MAKES A TRIUMPHANT RETURN

The Rich Ratio is *the simplest way to measure the amount of money you have in relation to the amount of money you need*. The system works regardless of your income level. If your Rich Ratio is greater than 1, you're rich, and if it's under 1, you've got room for improvement.

A quick reminder on how to determine your Rich Ratio:[8]

First, calculate your total monthly income net of taxes.

Then calculate your needs. To do this, simply use your projected monthly retirement budget. With these two numbers, our equation looks like this:

$$\text{Have} \div \text{Need} = \text{Rich Ratio}$$

Let's look at two very different retirees: a man named Tom and a woman named Theresa.

Tom never got married. He's been living—and loving—the bachelor's life since college. He has a pilot's license and a penchant for travel. He is expecting to spend $10,000 per month to support his jet-setting lifestyle during retirement. He is 65 and receiving Social Security ("SS") benefits ($2,000 per month), plus a modest pension from his early days working in telecom ($1,000 per month). Tom has also saved $1,000,000 in his 401(k).

Tom's "Have" = $2,000 SS + $1,000 pension + $3,750 [4.5% of his 401(k) on a monthly basis] = $6,750

Tom's "Need" = $10,000

Tom's Rich Ratio = $6,750 ÷ $10,000 = 0.675

While Tom might be a millionaire, considering his Rich Ratio is below 1, I wouldn't consider him "rich" at all.

Now let's take a look at Theresa's situation. Theresa's husband passed away a few years ago. She needs just $3,500 per month to live her vision of a good life. Her house is paid off, and she has very little debt. Once she retires, Theresa will receive $1,700 in SS benefits and $1,500 from her pension. She has also stashed away $400,000 in her 401(k).

Theresa's "Have" = $1,700 SS + $1,500 pension + $1,500 [4.5% of her 401(k) on a monthly basis] = $4,700

Theresa's "Need" = $3,500

Theresa's Rich Ratio = $4,700 ÷ $3,500 = 1.3

Theresa's "have" number is a lot lower than Tom's, but so is her "need," resulting in a much better Rich Ratio of 1.3. So even though Theresa has a smaller net worth (and less in retirement savings) than Tom, she is still much "richer" than Tom.

Theresa is on a road to a secure retirement, while Tom still has some work to do. He needs to reduce his planned retirement spending and/or boost his post-career income. A part-time job with an airline might earn Tom extra money and discounts on travel. Let's hope he won't be leaving happiness on a jet plane anytime soon.

IT'S NEVER TOO LATE . . .
BUT START NOW

As you may remember from Chapter 6—or maybe not, that was a long time ago—HROBs spend, on average, more time budgeting than UROBs. Retirees who reported never discussing their finances (zero hours per month) are two times more likely to end up in the unhappy camp, whereas happy retirees spend between one and two hours a month talking about their finances: retirement savings, mortgage balance, car payments, paying off debt, location for retirement, healthcare costs, and so on.

The happiest retirees are great about understanding the general shape of their monthly budget in a way that doesn't take a whole lot of time. There are many valuable resources for that. I use Vanguard's retirement expense worksheet.[9] You can fill it out online. Easy! Kiplinger's household budget worksheet is also great.[10] Consumer.gov has a PDF version if you prefer putting pencil to paper. It doesn't matter which one you use, it's just a matter of doing it. They're all good.

In Chapter 3, I talked about my TSL (Taxes, Savings, Life) budgeting approach: in preretirement, allocate 30 percent of your income for taxes, 20 percent for savings, and 50 percent for life, which includes both the stuff you have to do and the stuff you want to do (your core pursuits!). But in retirement, you no longer need to sock away that 20 percent because the time has come to spend it!

The cherry on top is that your taxes will usually decrease from the 30 percent range down to around 20 percent (or less). TSL becomes TL: taxes and life. That leaves you with a solid 80 percent plus: more money to spend on the things that truly bring you joy.

Maybe it's because I'm a financial advisor and witness first-hand the misguided guilt so many people have when it comes to spending, but I feel the need to reiterate what I said earlier. If you follow your budget, you get to do whatever you want. If your friend gives you a hard time for buying a new car because he still drives an old truck, that's his problem. And for what it's worth, he might be driving an old truck because he spends $10,000 a month on his horses. You don't know. His decisions aren't up to you, and yours aren't up to him.

Here's what I need you to hear: *it's never too late to save for retirement.*[11] Starting earlier doesn't necessarily mean you'll be happier, and starting later doesn't necessarily mean you'll be unhappy. You can start to save at any age and still become the Happiest Retiree on the Block. But the sooner you start, the better.

DEATH BY A THOUSAND SUBSCRIPTIONS

I want to end this chapter where we began: with the idea of *spending only on what brings you joy.*

What constitutes wasteful spending for you? For David Bach, it was lattes. A latte-and-scone-a-day habit may only cost you $5 to $10 each day, but that could end up costing you almost $1 million over 40 years. Is it really worth it?

For some people, the answer may be yes. Don't get between them and their coffee! Maybe that skinny soy chai latte and blueberry scone are how they like to start the day, or the winning formula for getting "in the zone" before a big project.

But for others, that latte is just an unexamined holdover from their college days when they had an early class. Those people are spending $5 to $10 each day on a caffeine habit that is bringing them no joy and really *is* a waste of money. That's almost $1 million swirling down the drain when you take the next 40 years into account.

But the latte is really just a metaphor. In today's world, wasteful spending can take many forms. Lately I've been thinking a lot about subscription services, which for me are the invisible deadly "lattes," the little incremental ways people get bled dry in ways they're not even consciously aware of.

It might be a gym membership you're not using or the five things you signed up for through iTunes that you've totally forgotten about. Multiple Amazon monthly subscriptions. The apps on your iPhone each siphoning between $2.99 and $12.99 a year. Your JibJab membership that automatically renews annually, even though you haven't sent a JibJab card since 2012. The subscription to HBO, Netflix, Showtime, or Amazon Prime you purchased so you could watch that one show . . . and the last season wrapped up years ago. *Game of Thrones* is over, and Daenerys isn't coming back. Let go.

What else? VIP memberships for food delivery services through DoorDash, Grubhub, Postmates, Caviar, and ChowNow that you no longer use. Do you really need that Audible subscription, even though you hardly ever listen to audiobooks? Because let me tell you: they are billing your card every month, regardless of the 47 James Patterson mystery novels sitting unread in your account.

Look, if you love a lotta lattes, drink your heart out. You have my permission, as long as you're prepared to give up something else. I think the more insidious "lattes" are the subscription services that suck us dry financially every month. As my friend David Bach would be the first to attest, that's the inverse of paying yourself first. Subscription services pay *them*selves first. Don't succumb to death by a thousand subscriptions. That money should be going toward a warm cuppa retirement happiness, topped with a fresh dollop of joy.

Join the Happiest Retirees Club

You made it. You now know the 10 financial and lifestyle habits that make HROBs tick, as well as dozens of other practices, choices, traits, preferences, and behaviors that can lead to a happy retirement.

But here's the thing: none of this stuff is black and white. That isn't how finances—or for that matter, life—work. It's not a matter of, "Oh, we should definitely pay off the mortgage, or we definitely shouldn't." "We should definitely take this next vacation, or we definitely shouldn't." "We should definitely let Johnny keep living at home for another six months, or we definitely shouldn't."

Yoda said, "There is no try." I say, "There is no *definitely*."

I'm not a Jedi master, but I've spent the last 20+ years studying HROBs and UROBs, so you might say I've been around the block. There is no perfect answer to any of these questions. What I like to say when I'm advising families through any sort of decision is: What would the happiest retiree do?

That's where a book like this comes in handy. At every fork in the road, with every choice big or small, we just want to make sure our happy habits outweigh the unhappy ones. These 10 habits help tip your retirement toward happiness. They are essentially keys to help you unlock the best financial and life decisions, leading to the highest levels of satisfaction.

Put another way: you can use this book and these habits as financial tiebreakers. Maybe you and your wife are at odds on whether you should pay off your mortgage. She says one thing; you say another. Just pull out *What the Happiest Retirees Know* and flip to Chapter 10. It's right there staring you in the face: a little chart showing that, as years to pay off a mortgage go down, happiness levels go up.

Now you have more information to make an informed decision. You've found your tiebreaker. If your financial profile fits the One-Third Rule, by all means write that check today.

For the most part, though, these habits are not rules. They are meant to be guidelines. Think of them as variables in an all-important equation:

$$\text{Money} + \text{Health} + \text{Connection} = \text{Happiness}$$

Remember those scary statistics I shared at the start of this book? Here's the scary recap: more than four out of five Americans either can't retire or won't be able to maintain their pre-retirement lifestyle when they do, meaning they will not have the financial security to support all the things they want to do in their golden years.[1] That means *fewer than one in five people* get to have a safe and secure retirement in which they're not constantly worried about running out of money.

I want you to count yourself among the one in five. I'll do you one better: I want you to be one of the lucky ones who's figured out how to have not just a secure retirement but a blissful, joyous one.

Adopting the habits in this book is not a guarantee of happiness. Happiness isn't a Whirlpool washing machine: it doesn't come with a guarantee. But here's the part that really gets me fired up. When you take all these happiness habits collectively—the money habits, the health habits, the social habits—they also lead to a higher probability that you will *be able to retire sooner* than most folks.

That's my great hope: that the habits in this book will make you happy and healthy in retirement, *and* get you there faster. It seems too good to be true. But that's exactly what my studies have shown. The men and women already practicing these financial and lifestyle habits are not only happier, they're ones who can retire one, three, five years sooner than they thought they could . . . which means they'll be even happier.

After years of digging into what the happiest retirees know, I want more than anything to share everything I've learned. That's why I created the Retire Sooner podcast with an ambitious goal: to help a million people retire at least a year earlier, creating *one million years of financial freedom and retirement happiness that didn't exist before*. With 10,000 baby boomers retiring every single day on average—that's 3.65 million baby boomers retiring annually in the next decade—it means we could help *over 36 million people retire early* over the next 10 years.

Told you it was ambitious. But I'm all in. I think we can get there. And how do we get there?

By practicing the financial and lifestyle habits of the happiest retirees.

I'm in my forties with four little kids. Retirement is still a ways off. But I put these habits into action every day. I've learned so much from the HROBs I've been lucky enough to work with. I use the habits in my own financial tiebreakers, asking myself, "What would the happiest retirees do? How can I have the financial foundation to be able to make better and better choices as I move forward in my life?"

It's a marathon, not a sprint. We're all going to mess up. We might even choose *not* to follow every single habit as a rule of law. Sometimes wonderful things can happen as a result. If I'd stuck to my guns about how the happiest retirees have on average 2.5 children, my wife and I wouldn't have our fourth and youngest son. I thank God for him every day.

For me, these habits simply nudge me to be better. How can I be more curious? Would touring the national parks or learning to sail be a fun core pursuit? Is it time to text my buddies for a golf date? What burns more calories, golf or curling? How often should my wife and I talk about our budget? Family staycation or go somewhere? Church or Sunday football? Tap water or full-fat mocha latte? Where are some places I could volunteer and really make a difference? How can I be a better friend, better husband, better son, better father?

And how can I be a better author, radio/podcast host, and investment strategist, both for the people I already work with and the ones I've yet to meet?

Studying America's happiest retirees is one of my core pursuits, but it's so much more than that. My mission is to continue to research, discover, and share these financial and lifestyle habits. It's part of my life's work to teach people how to have a secure, healthy, and joyful retirement—and to get you to a position of financial freedom sooner than you thought possible.

And if we can do that together? You as the reader, me as the author? Then I can't think of a better partnership. That's exactly why I wrote this book.

The conversation doesn't have to end here. I invite you to tune into our *Money Matters* radio show, which airs on 95.5 WSB Radio in Atlanta and on demand at wsbradio.com. Or drop in and listen to an episode of the Retire Sooner with Wes Moss podcast, available wherever you get your podcasts. Since you already know the happy retiree habits, I suggest starting with episode two: David Bach on Moving Overseas. If you like it, subscribe so you never miss an episode. If you *really* like it, leave a nice review and forward the podcast to a friend.

Same goes for this book: if you've found it helpful, share it with a friend or family member. Helping someone retire happily is a wonderful gift. Let me know if you're planning to give it as a present—I'd be happy to send you a signed copy.

And if you're a happy retiree, please share your story with me! I love getting letters and notes and pictures from happy retirees around the United States and on their adventures around the world. It totally lights me up and makes my day. Just go to WesMoss.com and drop me a line.

While you're there, I invite you to sit a spell. Take a couple of minutes to fill out the Happiness Questionnaire to see if you're on track to be a happy retiree.[2] Check out the Core Pursuit Finder to discover some new ways to nurture your curiosity, stoke your passions, and up your happiness game.[3]

My team and I are always available to answer your questions and hear your stories, which is easy to do through WesMoss.com. Happy retirees are our life's mission. This movement is sweeping across America—and we want you to be a part of it.

Retire soon.

Retire secure.

Retire healthy.

Retire joyously.

Be the Happiest Retiree on the Block.

Acknowledgments

Writing a book is always a difficult task, and finishing one is a true miracle. It starts with a nagging feeling that some mineral of information lodged underneath the mantle of my brain's core could possibly help people navigate their own lives. From there it takes a team of people to extract the data and process it into an informative and entertaining read. I'm lucky enough to work with the very best. I send them down into the mine, and they come back up with gold.

This book wouldn't be nearly as good without our team of writers and research analysts. Writing is like staring into the eyes of Thanos and therefore requires Avengers to win the battle. Bree Barton and Ryan Doolittle, the Tony Stark and Star-Lord of book publishing, are the only two storytellers who possess enough magical powers to make me enjoy a three-hour-long Zoom call.

The CIA research and analytics team, headed up by Connor Miller, painstakingly lived in spreadsheets to help all of us decipher the research data well enough to properly interpret the results. Ryan Ely has helped inspire me to continuously pursue the study of happy retirees and interpret their ways for others to emulate. Jeff Lloyd has helped turn reams of Excel data into actionable ideas.

The CIA marketing team, led by Mallory Boggs and Elizabeth Kelly, more than strongly encouraged me to forge ahead on this endeavor. Andrea Rizk enabled our message to spread to HROBs around the world. I'm grateful to this team for nudging me toward picking my research back up.

I would like to thank our entire team of rock stars at Capital Investment Advisors who are continuously guided by our firm's mission: Helping Families Find Happiness in Retirement. Our team showcases the essence of our company values: know your craft, be obsessed/passionate about what you do, do what is right, and every person matters. Much of our team at CIA also double on projects like the podcast and radio show.

The podcast is exhilarating and educational because of remarkable guests such as David Bach, Gretchen Rubin, Clark Howard, Dan Buettner, and Chris Gardner. The radio show is the country's longest-running, live, call-in investment and personal finance production thanks to all the fine people who keep listeners tuned to the right frequency.

I'd like to thank my real-life Jerry Maguire: my agent, Cindy Zigmund, who actually helped me start my book career when she was an editor at Dearborn. My editor, Casey Ebro, at McGraw Hill believed in me and brought this book to life.

I'd like to thank the loving folks we advise for sending the dozens of stories and pictures I've received over the last several years. Your letters and postcards from travels around the globe inspire us to continue to do the work we do, helping families find happiness in retirement. Thank you, Safari Sam, the Bands, and Round the World Robyn—you know who you are.

Finally, I want to thank my wife, Lynne, and our four boys, Ben, Jake, Luke, and Samuel, for all the love, support, and patience. You are my most cherished core pursuits.

Appendix: Your Handy Guide

The habits in this book are grouped into 10 chapters, each centered on a specific category. In every chapter are an abundance of individual practices, including the behaviors, preferences, and choices that the happiest retirees make. These decisions may be big—like how many kids you're going to have—or they may be seemingly insignificant, like going to a rock concert this weekend.

No one can observe every single one of these practices. I sure don't! The idea is to incorporate as many as you can into your daily, weekly, monthly, and yearly routines. The more of these you adopt, the better your chances of becoming the Happiest Retiree on the Block:

1. **HROBs have a minimum of $500,000 in liquid retirement savings.** That includes stocks, bonds, mutual funds, ETFs, crypto, cash, etc.—money you can easily access. Interestingly, having over $500,000 in liquid net worth doesn't necessarily mean a giant leap in happiness—there's a money-and-happiness plateau—so rest assured that you don't need to be a multimillionaire. While HROBs have an *average* liquid net worth of $874,479, getting to the *median* of $500,000 just might do the trick.

2. **Happy retirees have either paid off their mortgage or will soon.** Mortgage payoffs are hotly debated in the financial advising world, and people have vastly different

opinions. I can only tell you what I've seen from working with people for more than 20 years and conducting extensive research along the way: I believe the happiest retirees enter retirement either mortgage-free or with a payoff in sight (ideally within five years). They're breathing easily, without the ever-present specter of the bank hanging over their heads. To decide whether you can safely get rid of your mortgage, I recommend using the One-Third Rule: if you can pay off your mortgage using no more than one-third of your nonretirement savings, go for it.

3. **The happiest retirees have multiple streams of retirement income.** You're not looking for one formidable waterway. You want several tributaries flowing together to form a powerful life-sustaining river. Those tributaries could include multiple pensions, Social Security, rental properties, investment income, hobby income, or part-time work.

4. **Core pursuits are your hobbies on steroids—and the happiest retirees have at least 3.6 of them.** Unhappy retirees either don't have anything they enjoy doing when they're not at work, or they may halfheartedly engage in one or two hobbies on the weekends. Happy retirees, on the other hand, nurture their curiosity and sense of adventure, engaging wholeheartedly in at least 3.6 core pursuits. Bonus points if your chosen core pursuits also keep you active, healthy, and socially connected. If you're scratching your head wondering which core pursuits are for you, try the Core Pursuit finder on WesMoss.com!

5. **Among the top core pursuits are travel, volunteering, spending time with kids and grandkids, and a variety**

of exercise-oriented pursuits—including playing golf or tennis. In my data on America's happiest retirees, I've consistently seen these activities rise to the top. Many of them have a social aspect, which is crucial: travel exposes you to new places and new people, kids and grandkids keep you young, golf and tennis strengthen friendships *and* your fitness level, and volunteering gives you purpose and passion during your golden years.

6. **On average, happy retirees have 2.5 kids.** This is one of those "rules" that can be bent. Keep in mind I have four kids myself, so this was one guideline I was happy not to follow! Also, it's important to note that, according to my research, happiness in retirement doesn't necessarily go *down* after 2.5 kids. It just doesn't keep climbing.

7. **The very happiest of retirees live near at least half of their kids—and are less likely to support them financially.** If you want to be happy in retirement, your adult kids should live *near* you, not *with* you. My research makes it crystal clear that when parents fund their children's lifestyles or let them move back home for an extended period of time, their happiness levels can sharply decline. But retirees who live near at least half or more of their children are *two to five times* more likely to be happy.

8. **Overeducating your kids is overrated.** Studies have shown that education is generally a good thing—higher education is associated with longer life expectancies and various other indicators of health and happiness. However, when adult kids pile on multiple graduate and postgraduate degrees, it can have a negative impact on their parents' happiness.

9. **Kids should get married and get out.** This one's hard because unless you're a professional matchmaker, you probably can't make your kids fall in love. But the numbers don't lie: retirees are twice as likely to be unhappy if their adult children are still livin' that single life.

10. **Retirees are 4.5 times more likely to be unhappy if they're not married.** I'm not saying it's impossible to be an HROB if you're single, but you do have to work a lot harder to create a strong circle of support. If marriage isn't for you, make sure you invest in building many close relationships with family and friends.

11. **You can still be a happy retiree if you've gotten a divorce.** But only *one* divorce, mind you. Happiness levels don't dip with second marriages. Once you get to three and four marriages, however, you're less likely to be happy. But you get one marriage mulligan! Use with care.

12. **Happy retirees discuss money, but they don't obsess over it.** Happy retirees spend, on average, one or two hours a month having an honest, constructive conversation about money. Once you spend more than 3.5 hours a month, happiness levels start to decline. Likewise, retirees who reported never discussing their finances were twice as likely to be unhappy. The takeaway? Talk about your money, just don't talk it—or each other—to death.

13. **HROBs don't shy away from the bedroom.** My research showed that retirees who had sex less than once a month weren't happy campers. So at least once a month is good— but once a week is even better. Those who carved out several times a week for intimacy were twice as likely to be

happy. So turn the lights down low, put on some groovy music, and get it on!

14. **Retirees who attend a place of worship an average of once a week are 1.5 times more likely to be happy.** If you can make it to your church, synagogue, mosque, or temple most weeks, you're in great shape. I could be doing a better job of this myself. Think of your place of worship as a social epicenter—not a static building, but a dynamic community. It's harder to maintain social networks in retirement, so becoming active with your chosen place of worship gives you access to a group of people doing good works.

15. **HROBs both believe and give.** Most faith-based communities have ample opportunities for retirees looking to give their time, energy, resources, or all three to causes they believe in. Turn your beliefs into action, either by tithing and offering financial support, or by rolling up your sleeves and getting your hands dirty. You might offer to serve underprivileged children, food-insecure communities, women's shelters, people suffering from homelessness or mental illness, or an animal rescue. Go where you're called.

16. **The happiest retirees have at least three "CCs" (close connections) aka friends.** More is great, too! There is no happiness plateau when it comes to friendships. But you should try to have at least three, since that seems to be the inflection point: unhappy retirees have on average 2.6 CCs, whereas happy retirees have 3.6.

17. **Happy retirees make a conscious effort to see their close friends on a regular basis.** My research shows that seeing

those CCs once or twice a year just won't cut it. Aim for once a month, which leads to more retirement happiness. I highly recommend traveling with friends, something Lynne and I greatly enjoy doing. Even taking one trip a year with good friends makes you twice as likely to land in the HROB camp.

18. **The happiest retirees belong to at least one social group.** The kind of group doesn't matter, nor does it matter how organized it is. The HROBs I've worked with are in church groups, tennis teams, running and hiking groups, book clubs, civic engagement teams, and neighborhood cleanup crews. And it only takes one to move the needle: I found that being part of just one social group increases retirement happiness by almost double.

19. **Many of the happiest retirees go to concerts.** This was one of my favorite findings. HROBs love music, and they go out and enjoy it. There's even research that experiencing music may be the key to a longer lifespan. That and being a Galapagos tortoise. It doesn't matter if it's classical, pop, country, jazz, or rock.

20. **HROBs stay active, and they love what I call the *ings*.** These are low-cost, high-impact forms of exercise like walking, swimming, biking, jogging, running, and hiking. Happy retirees value their fitness, so they're less keen on the more passive *ing*s, like sitting around, watching TV, and eating ice cream. If you're looking for higher-octane ways to stay active, you might try tennis or badminton, which in one study were found to add 9.7 and 6.2 years, respectively, to life expectancy. Incredible!

21. **The happiest retirees care about what they eat.** While they're not always beholden to a specific diet, they stay away from constant takeout and junk food. Many HROBs are fans of the Mediterranean diet, which means they eat lots of fish, poultry, vegetables, fruits, whole grains, healthy fats, beans, and eggs—nothing too crazy. The important thing is, they make conscious choices about what, when, and how they eat.

22. **HROBs aren't teetotalers; they love a good glass of white wine or a tumbler of gin.** My data showed that retirees who had one or two drinks per day were just as happy as those who had zero drinks per day. So assuming there isn't some underlying issue or addiction, feel free to pour yourself a glass.

23. **Happy retirees live in nice houses but not McMansions.** Happiness does not rise in lockstep with square footage. When I first started researching retirement happiness back in 2013, the average HROB home value came out to around $355,000. Though thanks to the breathtaking increase in home values, that number is closer to $585,000 in 2021.

24. **HROBs don't downsize.** This is one of my newer findings. People may think retirement is the perfect time to downsize, but my data shows that happy retirees usually don't. They love their neighbors and have established themselves in their communities. Furthermore, they understand that their neighborhoods and networks are more important than four walls. And perhaps most importantly, they anticipate their kids and grandkids are going to come home to visit.

25. **Dividend investing is one of the most powerful tools in the HROB's toolkit.** Stock dividend income wins against bond income by an incredibly large margin, and has proven to grow at twice the rate of inflation over the better part of market history. HROBs know this, and they use dividend income for recurring cash flow they can actually live on.

26. **The happiest retirees know that investing is less about perfection and more about participation.** Unhappy retirees chase the "perfect" stock, which they're determined to buy at the "perfect" time. That's a recipe for failure. I like to tell people that if you have time, you've got time. Perfect is the enemy of the good.

27. **HROBs are tomorrow investors, not today investors.** They don't make decisions based on emotion, and they're not fueled by fear or panic. Instead, they look at the bigger picture, understanding that volatility is actually their friend. The happiest retirees know how to find a strategy and stick to it. They're in it for the long haul.

28. **The happiest retirees have unlocked the power of the 4 Percent *Plus* Rule.** This used to be the 4 Percent Rule, but these days it's sporting a new look. Applying this rule is the easiest and simplest way to know how much you can safely spend during retirement—and it's the guiding principle for what percentage of your retirement portfolio you can withdraw yearly, adjusted for inflation, to ensure you will never run out of money.

29. **HROBs know how to use the Rich Ratio.** Divide how much you have (your total monthly income net) by how much you need (your projected monthly retirement

budget). If your Rich Ratio is greater than 1, you're rich. If it's under 1, you've got room for improvement.

30. **The happiest retirees are masters of the middle.** They're not lavish spenders, but they don't penny pinch either. They know how to both save and spend responsibly. HROBs don't let themselves get overextended. While they may have had times in their lives when they were carrying credit card debt or struggling financially, they always find their way back to center.

Disclaimer

The views, thoughts, and opinions expressed in this book belong solely to the author, and not necessarily to the author's employer, Capital Investment Advisors, LLC. This publication is provided for informational purposes only and should not be regarded as personalized investment advice or a reflection of the performance of Capital Investment Advisors, LLC, or its clients. Investors should seek advice from a qualified financial advisor about their specific situation prior to implementing an investment strategy. The information provided is not an offer or solicitation of any product or service.

Current and future markets may differ significantly from those illustrated herein. Past performance is not a guarantee of future returns.

Any changes to assumptions that may have been made in preparing this material (e.g., the retiree surveys) could have a material impact on the information presented. There is no representation or warranty as to the current accuracy, reliability, or completeness of nor liability for decisions based on such information, and it should not be relied on as such.

Investing in securities involves risk of loss. Equity investments are subject to market risk or the risk that stocks will decline in response to such factors as adverse company news or industry developments or a general economic decline. Dividend yield is one component of performance and should not be the only consideration for investment. Dividends are not guaranteed and will fluctuate. Among other things, fixed income investments are subject to interest rate risk, reinvestment risk, and inflation risk.

Notes

Preface

1. http://content.time.com/time/magazine/article/0,9171,2019628,00.html.
2. https://www.princeton.edu/~deaton/downloads/deaton_kahneman_high _income_improves_evaluation_August2010.pdf.
3. https://www.wsj.com/articles/the-case-against-early-retirement-115558 99000.

Chapter 1

1. https://www.financialplanningassociation.org/article/journal/FEB21-right -sizing-retirement.
2. https://www.chrishogan360.com/retirement/10-frightening-retirement -stats-that-should-scare-you-into-action.
3. https://www.wesmoss.com/news/the-power-of-investing-in-dividends -generating-income-from-stock-dividends-vs-bond-interest/. Please note that investing always involves risk, and there is no guarantee that the S&P 500 will perform as well as it has in the past. From Investopedia: "What Is the S&P 500 Index? The S&P 500 Index, or the Standard & Poor's 500 Index, is a market-capitalization-weighted index of the 500 largest publicly-traded companies in the U.S. It is not an exact list of the top 500 U.S. companies by market capitalization because there are other criteria to be included in the index. The index is widely regarded as the best gauge of large-cap U.S. equities." https://www.investopedia.com/terms/s/sp500.asp.
4. https://www.cnn.com/shows/anthony-bourdain-parts-unknown/.
5. https://www.wesmoss.com/news/if-you-want-to-live-longer-drink-champagne -and-eat-chocolate/.
6. https://www.wsj.com/articles/the-case-against-early-retirement-115558 99000.
7. https://crr.bc.edu/working-papers/how-does-delayed-retirement-affect -mortality-and-health/.
8. https://www.youtube.com/watch?v=8pqhd_O1Feo.

Chapter 2

1. https://www.ajc.com/business/personal-finance/wes-moss-why-500-000 -key-figure-retirement-planning/4wch2SNjqWmLl4WHlL33pO/.
2. https://www.princeton.edu/~deaton/downloads/deaton_kahneman_high _income_improves_evaluation_August2010.pdf.

3. https://www.wesmoss.com/news/living-near-but-not-with-the-kids-and
-other-important-rules-for-retirement-happiness/.
4. https://www.bostonglobe.com/lifestyle/2015/12/13/close-grandparent
-grandchild-relationships-have-healthy-benefits/kxL8AnugpVBKknDuz
HZDKO/story.html.
5. https://www.wesmoss.com/news/kids-on-the-payroll-the-biggest-retirement
-problem-no-one-talks-about/.
6. https://www.cnn.com/2020/09/04/us/children-living-with-parents
-pandemic-pew/index.html.

Chapter 3

1. https://www.nytimes.com/2006/12/12/science/all-but-ageless-turtles-face
-their-biggest-threat-humans.html.
2. https://andrewsteele.co.uk/ageless/.
3. https://dqydj.com/sp-500-return-calculator/.
4. https://dqydj.com/wilshire-reit-index-return-calculator/.
5. https://www.marketwatch.com/story/suze-orman-says-you-need-5-million
-to-retire-thats-nonsense-2019-01-15.
6. https://www.wesmoss.com/news/how-to-use-1000-bucks-a-month-rule-to
-plan-for-your-retirement/.
7. https://www.wesmoss.com/news/why-you-need-to-prepare-for-the
-retirement-grey-zone/.
8. https://www.yourwealth.com/retirement-timeline/.
9. https://www.wesmoss.com/news/how-to-maximize-social-security-income
-in-retirement/.
10. https://www.wesmoss.com/news/companies-with-great-benefits-for-part
-time-workers/.
11. https://www.wesmoss.com/news/creating-income-in-retirement-through
-investments/.
12. https://www.yourwealth.com/retirement-timeline/.
13. https://www.fidelity.com/viewpoints/personal-finance/plan-for-rising
-health-care-costs.

Chapter 4

1. https://www.wesmoss.com/news/what-are-core-pursuits/.
2. https://en.wikipedia.org/wiki/Michel_Alaux.
3. https://www.wesmoss.com/news/why-its-critical-to-find-your-core-pursuits
-before-retirement/.
4. https://www.wesmoss.com/news/10-meaningful-volunteer-opportunities
-in-retirement/.
5. https://www.nationalservice.gov/newsroom/press-releases/2019/volunteering
-helps-keep-seniors-healthy-new-study-suggests.

6. https://clark.com/personal-finance-credit/investing-retirement/national-parks-challenge/.
7. https://www.wesmoss.com/news/what-you-need-to-do-the-last-five-years-before-retirement/.
8. https://www.wesmoss.com/news/15-of-the-best-senior-discounts-in-america/.
9. https://www.wesmoss.com/news/senior-pass-with-lifetime-access-to-national-parks-is-about-to-get-a-major-price-increase/.
10. https://www.wesmoss.com/core-pursuit-finder/.

Chapter 5

1. https://www.cnn.com/2020/09/04/us/children-living-with-parents-pandemic-pew/index.html.
2. https://www.wesmoss.com/news/kids-on-the-payroll-the-biggest-retirement-problem-no-one-talks-about/.
3. https://www.cnn.com/2020/09/04/us/children-living-with-parents-pandemic-pew/index.html.
4. https://www.pewresearch.org/fact-tank/2020/09/04/a-majority-of-young-adults-in-the-u-s-live-with-their-parents-for-the-first-time-since-the-great-depression/.
5. https://www.pewresearch.org/social-trends/2019/10/23/majority-of-americans-say-parents-are-doing-too-much-for-their-young-adult-children/.

Chapter 6

1. https://news.osu.edu/divorce-drops-a-persons-wealth-by-77-percent-study-finds/.
2. https://www.wesmoss.com/news/how-money-impacts-marital-happiness/.
3. https://www.marketwatch.com/story/why-68-of-people-would-rather-talk-about-their-weight-than-money-2018-01-25.
4. https://www.huffpost.com/entry/5-stresses-of-marriage-and-how-you-navigate_b_3187099.
5. https://www.wesmoss.com/news/the-happiest-retirees-dont-obsess-over-they-discuss-their-money/.
6. https://www.wesmoss.com/news/how-money-impacts-marital-happiness/.

Chapter 7

1. https://www.ajc.com/business/wes-moss-how-religion-fits-into-retirement-happiness/sTPVnDFL7Fbx5Ckt4G33OO/.
2. https://www.pewforum.org/2019/10/17/in-u-s-decline-of-christianity-continues-at-rapid-pace/.
3. https://www.bluezones.com/exploration/loma-linda-california/.

4. https://www.fidelitycharitable.org/.
5. https://www.schwabcharitable.org/.

Chapter 8

1. https://my.clevelandclinic.org/health/treatments/12578-kangaroo-care.
2. https://www.webmd.com/balance/news/20180504/loneliness-rivals-obesity
   -smoking-as-health-risk.
3. https://www.ajc.com/business/wes-moss-being-social-butterfly-might-help
   -you-live-longer/f6AjlX8BM2aXXxGgou4IqL/.
4. https://www.wsj.com/articles/the-case-against-early-retirement-11555
   899000.
5. file:///C:/Users/dooli/Downloads/SSRN-id2867594.pdf OR https://papers
   .ssrn.com/sol3/papers.cfm?abstract_id=2867594.
6. https://www.wsj.com/articles/the-case-against-early-retirement-1155
   5899000.
7. https://www.wesmoss.com/news/concert-lovers-rejoice-experiencing-live
   -music-may-be-the-key-to-a-longer-lifespan/.
8. https://www.newsweek.com/going-concerts-can-help-you-live-longer
   -according-new-study-863628.
9. https://en.wikipedia.org/wiki/Moai_(social_support_groups).
10. https://www.healthline.com/nutrition/blue-zones#TOC_TITLE_HDR_3.

Chapter 9

1. https://www.instagram.com/tv/B_NkcbTgVfy.
2. https://www.mayoclinicproceedings.org/article/S0025-6196(18)30538-X
   /fulltext.
3. https://www.wesmoss.com/news/why-is-tennis-so-good-for-you/.
4. https://www.wsj.com/articles/SB1000142405297020355060457435965 29
   93619032.
5. https://www.kidzworld.com/article/4527-tiger-woods-biography/.
6. https://time.com/collection/guide-to-happiness/4870796/dog-owners
   -benefits/.
7. https://olympics.nbcsports.com/2020/05/05/michael-phelps-calories
   -swimming/.
8. https://www.wesmoss.com/news/if-you-want-to-live-longer-drink
   -champagne-and-eat-chocolate/.
9. https://whole30.com/.
10. https://www.atlantamealprep.com/.
11. https://www.wesmoss.com/news/if-you-love-to-travel-and-drink-gin-this-is
    -the-part-time-job-for-you/.
12. https://www.wesmoss.com/news/if-you-want-to-live-longer-drink-champagne
    -and-eat-chocolate/.

13. https://www.healthline.com/nutrition/12-benefits-of-meditation#1.-Reduces -stress.

Chapter 10

1. https://www.wesmoss.com/news/pay-off-mortgage-important-factors -consider/.
2. https://fred.stlouisfed.org/series/CSUSHPISA.
3. https://www.amazon.com/Nest-Bright-Early-Playtime-Books/dp/037 583267X.

Chapter 11

1. https://www.health.harvard.edu/staying-healthy/understanding-the-stress -response.
2. https://www.wesmoss.com/news/how-to-control-your-fear-of-investing/.
3. From 1980 through June 30, 2020, this study showed that *cumulatively*, bond interest totaled $25,117, while stock dividends totaled $76,230. From a *current income* perspective by 2020, stock dividends were more than 18 times that of bond interest per year ($5,724 vs. $311). Please note, there is no guarantee that stocks and bonds will perform as they have in the past.
4. https://www.wesmoss.com/news/why-we-feel-the-pain-of-loss-more-than -the-joy-of-gains/.
5. https://www.ajc.com/business/wes-moss-why-volatility-our-friend/cdoos CQtoFheC0dxplujxM/.

Chapter 12

1. https://davidbach.com/latte-factor-backup/.
2. https://www.investor.gov/financial-tools-calculators/calculators/compound -interest-calculator.
3. https://www.barrons.com/articles/the-originator-of-the-4-retirement-rule -thinks-its-off-the-mark-he-says-it-now-could-be-up-to-4-5-51611410402.
4. https://www.wsj.com/articles/forget-the-4-rule-rethinking-common -retirement-beliefs-1518172201.
5. https://www.forbes.com/sites/wadepfau/2016/04/19/the-4-rule-and-the -search-for-a-safe-withdrawal-rate/.
6. https://www.winnebago.com/models/product/motorhomes/minnie-winnie.
7. https://www.ajc.com/business/wes-moss-finding-the-formula-for-happy -retirement/r2HEjrYYLqCEjLfZOpuKAJ/.
8. https://www.ajc.com/lifestyles/wes-moss-figure-out-your-rich-ratio-help -plan-for-retirement/3MRa0Xxzha6Da1seugOVQN/.
9. https://investor.vanguard.com/retirement/income/retirement-planning -worksheet.
10. https://www.kiplinger.com/kiplinger-tools/spending/t007-s001-budgeting -worksheet-a-household-budget-for-today-a/index.php.

11. https://www.ajc.com/business/wes-moss-never-too-late-save-for-retirement
    /t0NU8iz7atPDFSxUAIrqmI/.

Conclusion
 1. https://www.financialplanningassociation.org/article/journal/FEB21-right
    -sizing-retirement.
 2. https://www.wesmoss.com/happiness-questionnaire/.
 3. https://www.wesmoss.com/core-pursuit-finder/.

Index

Unhappiest Retiree on the Block
(UROBs), *(cont'd)*
money influencing, 21–22
pretend rich of, 27

V

Vacation homes, 172
for happiness, 173–174
of HROBs, 171
secondary gathering places for,
173–174
Vacations, 11, 71
Veterinary medicine, xiii–xiv
Volunteering, 62, 109, 231, 233
accomplishment feelings from, 122
charitable activities in, 123–124, 140
in community, 66–69
for HROBs, 117
opportunities for, 124–125
as win-win situation, 68

W

Wall Street Journal, xii–xiii, 207–208
Wealthy people
Amish Americans contrasted with, xi
divorce influencing, 100

power and, 21
success and, 20
UROBs pretending to be, 27
Whole30 diet, 157
Wine clubs, 160
Withdrawal rates
factors of, 211–212
in financial planning, 208
increasing, 208
during retirement, 213
Witness (film), ix
Woods, Tiger, 153

Y

You Can Retire Sooner Than You Think
(Moss, W.), xi–xii, 22, 27
cooking and, 156, 195
core pursuits in, 59–62
4 Percent Rule in, 206, 211–212
mortgage payoff and, 44
Rich Ratio in, 46
Young adults, 83–84

Z

Zagorsky, Jay, 100

About the Author

 **Wes Moss is** a man on a mission. The Atlanta-based Certified Financial Planner™ and money educator has devoted his professional life to helping Americans understand how they can retire sooner than they think. Wes is a managing partner at Capital Investment Advisors (CIA), a fee-only investment firm that has over $3 billion in assets under management (as of March 15, 2021). As the company's Chief Investment Strategist, he leads a team of financial advisors who share a common goal: to help thousands of clients embrace the dream of retiring sooner and happier. A passionate financial educator, Moss uses every available platform to teach others how they, too, can retire on their own terms.

In addition to *What the Happiest Retirees Know*, Moss is the author of three other books, including the bestselling *You Can Retire Sooner Than You Think*. Moss is the creator and host of Retire Sooner, a top financial podcast focused on helping one million people retire one year sooner. He is also the host of *Money Matters*, the country's longest-running, weekly, call-in radio show on Atlanta's historic 95.5 WSB. Moss has been the financial columnist for the *Atlanta Journal-Constitution* for more than a decade, editor of WesMoss.com, a frequent guest and resource for national media outlets, and a sought-after speaker for conferences and events.

His accomplishments have earned him both national and local recognition. Each year from 2014 to 2018, *Barron's* magazine named Moss as one of America's top 1,200 Financial Advisors in its annual financial advisor rankings. In 2019 and 2020, *Barron's* recognized Moss among the top 100 Independent Financial Advisors in America. In 2021, *Forbes* magazine honored Moss in its annual rankings as a Best-In-State Wealth Advisor, listed at #2 in the state of Georgia. Also in 2021, *Atlanta Magazine* named Moss among Atlanta's 500 Most Powerful Leaders.

Before joining Capital Investment Advisors, Moss worked for UBS Financial Services in its Atlanta office. He holds a degree in economics from the University of North Carolina at Chapel Hill.

Moss lives in Atlanta with his wife, Lynne, and their four boys. He is an avid golfer and enjoys coaching his boys' lacrosse teams.

To find out more about Wes, please visit WesMoss.com.

Because learning changes everything.®